KARATE

BASIC CONCEPTS AND SKILLS

KARATE

BASIC CONCEPTS AND SKILLS

CHARLES ROY SCHROEDER

Memphis State University

BILL WALLACE

World Professional Karate Champion
1974 and 1975

ADDISON-WESLEY PUBLISHING COMPANY

Reading, Massachusetts • Menlo Park, California • London • Amsterdam • Don Mills, Ontario • Sydney

ISBN 0-201-06837-0
CDEFGHIJ-AL-79876

PREFACE

The term *karate* is a Japanese word meaning "empty hand." It refers to a type of unarmed self-defense that developed in the Orient over a period of thousands of years. Only in recent years has karate become popular in the United States and throughout the rest of the Western world.

Although there is wide variety in karate styles, those practiced in Japan, Korea, and Okinawa are by far the most prevalent in the West. Fortunately, these styles are similar enough to permit one basic book to be written that can be utilized for all of the karate systems.

The precise way one utilizes one's karate training depends upon personal interests and needs. Some participate chiefly for the relaxation or physical fitness benefits, others for the joy of movement and the kinesthetically beautiful feeling that it elicits. Still others seek the protective capability gained from the self-defense training, and there are increasing numbers of individuals who desire to compete in the *sport* of karate. This diversity in meeting personal needs is the primary reason for the phenomenal world-wide growth in interest in karate.

As in any athletic endeavor, it is impossible for one to achieve his or her *potential* in karate without individual training. It follows that no publication can completely take the place of a qualified instructor. However, using this book, one should be able to master a variety of karate stances, punches, strikes, kicks, and blocks, while simultaneously increasing his or her strength, stamina, and flexibility to a degree that will permit effective utilization of the karate skills. Further, by working up through the progressive levels of sparring shown one can learn to safely practice these skills against an opponent in preparation for the time when self-defense may be necessary against an actual assailant.

While this book is invaluable to persons who have no access to a qualified karate school, it will also be of considerable benefit to those who are fortunate enough to have an instructor. By providing the beginner with the basic knowledge and understanding of karate history, philosophy, principles, and skills, this book saves many hours of instructor time, thus allowing the instructor to devote more time to giving personal attention to his or her students on an individual level.

A *unique* facet of this book, which will benefit the expert as well as the novice, is the chapter dealing with fundamental principles of movement as they apply to karate. Instruction in subsequent chapters is based upon these principles. Students, therefore, not only gain a knowledge of *how* to execute the required skills but *why* they are performed in a particular way. As a result, their learning is not based merely upon rote memory and blind acceptance of traditional methods, but upon an *understanding* of the underlying mechanics dealing with balance, force, and motion. This approach to training prepares one to *creatively* adjust to combative situations that may occur; it is this creativity that elevates karate to its classification as a martial *art*. Karate participation based upon understanding and creativity involves a dynamic integration of the mind and body, resulting in an experience which is infinitely more stimulating and satisfying than either physical or mental experiences alone.

A recognition of the value of knowing WHY in addition to HOW also guided the presentation of the chapter dealing with *warming-up* and *stretching*. The benefits and physiological principles underlying these activities are discussed before specific exercises are listed and before a generalized warming-up and stretching program is offered. Deviation from the suggested program to meet individual requirements is encouraged; understanding the basic principles allows one to do so intelligently.

Because this is a beginning instructional book, the more esoteric *spiritual* facet of karate has not received as much overt emphasis as have the *physical* and *intellectual* aspects. It was felt that many persons might be "turned off" by a lengthy discourse on this topic in the initial stages of training. The need for an aura of spirituality surrounding one's karate activity, however, subtly pervades the entire book and is indicative of its significance in this potentially dangerous activity. As one becomes increasingly proficient, the need for one to exercise strict discipline and responsibility increases correspondingly. Still, attitudes of respect and consideration for others *must* be stressed as early as the first karate session.

Along with meeting other criteria, to advance from one skill level to another, one must satisfactorily perform at least one karate form (*kata*). Each kata is a kind of "training dance" devised to give the student an opportunity to display a variety of karate stances and techniques in an organized routine that approximates actual combat. Naturally, the forms become more difficult as one progresses up the ladder of karate proficiency. All demand a great deal of concentration and effort, because each "dance" must be flawlessly executed.

The kata chosen for this book is the *pinan chodan*. It is traditionally designated as the first form. There are variations among the different karate styles in the first form but the variations are slight. Because novices normally have difficulty in understanding the proper execution of a kata, the first form has been presented in a series of three hundred precisely drawn and sequentially arranged figures. Both front and back views are shown for additional clarification.

Although there are many values associated with karate training, the authors hope most of all that participants will find it a source of joy, and that they will become skillful, powerful, and secure enough to be gentle, considerate, and peaceful.

Memphis, Tennessee
December 1975

C.R.S.
B.W.

ACKNOWLEDGMENTS

While it is impossible to acknowledge everyone who has in some way contributed to the completion of this publication, we must recognize those most directly involved.

Gil Michael, Director of Memphis State University's Photo Services, and Brack Walker, Chairman of the Department of Graphic Design, are gratefully acknowledged for extending technical advice and for providing the facilities of their respective departments. Due to their help, Dr. Schroeder was able to take the photographs and draw the hundreds of illustrations that appear throughout the book. Rodney Puckett is credited with taking the cover photograph.

Judith Schroeder devoted many "fun-filled" hours to typing the manuscript and assisting with the editing. Her patience is appreciated as much as her work.

The models for the photographs and drawings were Ricardo Nuñez Bentz, Sherry Burton, Nam Cho, Loyce Jan Graham, Rodney Puckett, Charles Schroeder, Gail Simpson, John Steinhouse, David Teague, Bill Wallace, Dr. Chris Waser, and Will Wright.

Hagen Koo and Dr. Peter Takayama of Memphis State University, along with Nam Cho, assisted in the preparation of the Glossary.

Special recognition must be given to Gail Simpson. Because of her involvement in nearly every phase of manuscript preparation, she may almost be considered the third author.

CONTENTS

3

WARM-UP AND STRETCHING ACTIVITIES

4

BASIC PRINCIPLES OF KARATE MOVEMENT

5

KARATE STANCES AND TECHNIQUES

6

SPARRING AND SELF-DEFENSE

7

THE FIRST KATA

1 KARATE – PAST, PRESENT, AND FUTURE

HISTORY OF KARATE

Karate is a system of unarmed combat. Until the 1950's it was practiced solely in oriental and Far Eastern cultures. Since then it has gained such widespread attention that the entire world has become familiar with it. Karate's popularity in the United States has been furthered by the many public appearances by experts on television, demonstrations, tournaments, as well as through numerous books and magazines. Still, there are thousands interested in karate who do not understand its underlying principles, particularly its philosophical and spiritual basis. Indeed, a number of unqualified karate instructors have given such an erroneous impression of the skill that many viewers believe that it is either a brutal method of killing people or an esoteric form of magic that gives practitioners enormous power to destroy anything within their reach. This inaccurate and unfortunate concept of karate has been perpetuated by the many karate students and teachers who have little knowledge of the art's beginnings and development. These persons are severely handicapped in pursuing and teaching karate.

To fully understand the philosophy of karate, it is imperative to have a knowledge of karate's historical development. Some students have learned the art for the sake of "being tough." This is not the purpose of karate. The origin and development of today's karate, though obscured somewhat by time, will be presented here in a more accurate perspective. From this kind of approach one should better understand the purposes of karate and how its techniques evolved into the art form of today.

Egypt

The oldest records concerning unarmed combat are the hieroglyphics from the Egyptian pyramids where Egypt's military men, in about 4000 B.C. (Old Kingdom), used fighting techniques that resemble modern boxing. Other pictures portraying something akin to boxing and wrestling turned up in the ruins of Sumer in Mesopotamia (about 3000 B.C.). These fighting techniques crossed over to Greece by way of Crete, and were described by Homer in the twenty-third book of the *Iliad*. Matches then were rough affairs terminated often by the death of one of the participants.

Though a distinction existed between wrestling and boxing in those early times, such irregularities as striking one's opponent in what was supposed to be a wrestling match or strangling him in a so-called boxing match were common. By combining the two types of fighting, the Greeks devised an activity in which no such thing as a foul existed and any part of the body could be used as a weapon. Though the Greeks themselves soon found this sport too cruel and abandoned it, it was revived under the Roman Empire. This competition was similar to karate in its physical aspects.

India

Although the precise origin of karate as an organized system of self-defense is undetermined, most experts agree that, as a martial *art*, it had its beginnings in India thousands of years ago where it reached a high degree of sophistication. Indian folklore, history, dance, and drama are replete with stories of individual warriors, princes, and gods who accomplished incredible battlefield feats with their bare hands. Karate forms can also be found in many works of art, particularly in ancient temple sculptures where warriors are shown in positions nearly identical to those employed in karate today. This is not to say that there has been no further development in karate since those early times.

India's role as the birthplace of karate may be a surprise to many since Mahatma Gandhi's nonviolent struggle for independence led to the popular belief that India has always been antimilitaristic. This is not true; warfare was, in fact, a very significant aspect of early Indian culture. In pre-Christian times, there were many kingdoms in India vying with each other for supremacy. For this reason, warfare was thrust upon the people and many types of combat were developed out of necessity.

A warrior class called the "Kshatriya," whose members were comparable to the Japanese samurai and the European knight, were the dominant group in Indian society. Despite the difficulty in documenting the evolution of a karate-like art at such an early date, experts agree that at least one early fighting style was developed by the Kshatriya.

Written proof of a bare-handed type of fighting art was first stated in the Buddhist chronicle, *Lotus Sutra* (not to be confused with *Kama Sutra* which deals with a much different but still fascinating and delightful physical activity). Mention was made of pugilism, which is the practice of fighting with the fists. The chronicle further reveals that a type of unarmed combat existed even before the writing of *Lotus Sutra*.

Reference was also made to a fighting art called "nata." According to a Sanskrit-English dictionary, "nata" meant "a manly character; a dancer or performer." This is significant because modern karate has, as one of its bases, prearranged exercises which resemble dancing but are, in fact, practical defensive movements against one or more opponents. To the untrained eye these exercises appear to be dancing, but in actuality they are the foundations of a fighting art. Chapter Seven shows a basic karate form (or kata) which clearly reveals the dance-combative relationship.

India also appears to have developed another bare-handed fighting style, "Vajramushti," which is translated to mean "one whose clenched fist. . . ." The techniques are similar to the punches used in modern karate.

China

It was an Indian Buddhist monk named Bodhidharma who introduced karate techniques into China. Ironically, this was not at all his objective. He decided to go to China because he was not satisfied with the way Buddhism was being taught outside India (Buddhism, incidentally, also originated in India). Though the accounts of his travels and activities vary with different works, the most reliable sources indicate Bodhidharma arrived in China around 520 A.D.

Bodhidharma eventually received an audience with the Emperor and obtained permission to reside at the Shaolin-ssu Monastery in Hohon Province. This location was to become the birthplace of karate.

Upon arrival at the Shaolin Temple, Bodhidharma found the monks in poor physical condition due to inactivity resulting from hours of kneeling and meditation. Like many people, before and since, he sensed the intricate relationship between the body, mind, and spirit. Therefore he began teaching these Buddhist monks the system of integrated physical and mental discipline embodied in the Indian *I-Chin-Sutra* which he had been taught as a youngster while a member of the aforementioned Kshatriya. In later years, his exercises were further developed and integrated with various forms of Chinese unarmed combat and became what is known today as Shaolin Temple Boxing or Shaolin ch'uan fa (Chinese karate).

One may wonder why a Buddhist monk whose chief concern was to cultivate the minds and spirits of his followers so that enlightenment could be achieved, would initiate a system that was to become a brutally effective method of combat. Some historians claim that Bodhidharma never intended his system to be employed as a violent form of fighting but merely a form of exercise for improving the state of the monks' physical fitness. Other historians believe he instituted the activity so that the unarmed monks would be able to defend themselves against bandits who plagued the countryside and who were not above violating the sanctity of religion. There is no documentation to suggest that Bodhidharma intended his system to become a basis for *offensive* combat. In fact, for centuries it was taught in strict secrecy and only to the monks. Later, neighboring farmers were taught the skills so they too could protect themselves against marauding bandits.

The development of the Shaolin style of unarmed combat has a complex history. Although Bodhidharma first developed Shaolin *ch'uan fa*, his original eighteen techniques later evolved to a total of seventy-two. Expansion and sophistication of the techniques were achieved through the efforts of a ch'uan fa master named Ch'ueh Yuan Shangejen. He verified the existence of Bodhidharma's eighteen movements and included many of them in his own style. After Ch'ueh had spent some time spreading and popularizing the expanded form of Shaolin ch'uan fa, he traveled to Shensi Province where he met another martial artist named Li. These two men further developed the Shaolin Ch'uan fa to a total of 170 movements. It is only fair to state that many styles of karate-like techniques existed in China before the arrival of Bodhidharma. It should be stressed, however, that the Indian monk was apparently the first to give the activity its underlying basis of spiritualism that is such an integral part of karate today.

Secret societies have always played an important part in the history of karate in China. These societies generally worked for the betterment of the country. When hatred of the Western domination of China reached its peak in 1900, the karate societies were in the forefront of the resulting "Boxer Rebellion." The term "Boxer," incidentally, was first applied to the ch'uan fa (karate) practitioners by Westerners in China when they saw a similarity between ch'uan fa and their own brand of pugilism.

The 1900 uprising served to attract multitudes of Chinese, both young and old, into bands of activists who practiced numerous forms of ch'uan fa. In the West today, ch'uan fa is more popularly known as Chinese Kempo Boxing. Although the actual degree of ch'uan fa combat used in the war was slight, both the aristocracy and the peasantry seemed to have been mesmerized by the ch'uan fa performer and believed that they could overcome the well-armed Western soldiers with this weaponless art. As it turned out, most of the fighting by both sides was carried out with firearms and not with ch'uan fa.

Southeast Asia

Karate techniques appear to have flowed from China to neighboring Southeast Asia. In Cambodia, for instance, the statues and wall paintings from ancient times show the influence of the ch'uan fa of China. The probable reason for this influence was the peaceful relationship that had long existed between the two kingdoms. This meant that Chinese travelers and merchants probably visited Cambodia for trading purposes. Ch'uan fa undoubtedly followed as a form of exercise and self-defense.

The land now known as Viet Nam had for two thousand years, and until recently, owed its allegiance to China. Indeed, during one of China's expansion periods, Viet Nam was annexed (111 B.C.) and became part of the "Middle Kingdom." Undoubtedly the Chinese were instrumental in introducing ch'uan fa to Viet Nam; but, through a complexity that is typical of history, Japan was also involved in the development of karate in the Indochina area during World War II.

Although Thailand (formerly Siam) is the sole country in Southeast Asia to escape some type of colonialism, her customs still bear a remarkable resemblance to both Indian and Chinese cultures. The Thai art of "Kick Boxing," for example, is much like karate except that the boxer wears protective gloves. Apparently, ch'uan fa had some effect on the development of this sport, but it is impossible to document its specific influence.

Strong evidence exists to support the belief that both China and India gave Indonesia its earliest exposures to organized systems of unarmed combat. Since Chinese, Arab, Malay, and Filipino pirates periodically attacked the Indonesian people, such training was of utmost importance for protection of property and of life itself.

Eventually, many styles of karate evolved in Indonesia. All forms were localized, mainly in the villages, and were considered the property of that village. Only rarely were they taught to an outsider.

Okinawa

Of all the countries that have contributed to the evolution of the art of modern karate, tiny Okinawa was one of the most influential. It is generally accepted that Okinawa was first inhabited by shipwrecked survivors of vicious typhoons. These survivors were diplomats, priests, and scholars traveling to Japan from China. Certainly, some of the Chinese survivors must have been skilled in various systems of unarmed combat, including ch'uan fa; most Buddhist monks were trained in such techniques. The Japanese encyclopedia, *Sekai Dai-Huakkajiten*, states that karate skills were probably brought to Okinawa from China during the T'ang dynasty (A.D. 618-906). Subsequently, such skills evolved into a style of unarmed combat known as "tode," based solely on the use of the hands.

Obviously the growth of karate to its present state has been quite complex, and much of what is accepted as history is actually little more than conjecture. However, the year 1609 stands out as a most important and accurate date. Because Okinawa failed to supply Japan with the necessary materials for her abortive attack against China in 1592, the militaristic Japanese Satsuma clan of Southern Kyushu marched on Okinawa in 1609. All Okinawan weapons were confiscated, and a ban on the possession of all weapons and metals was proclaimed. Much bitterness naturally arose from this severe oppression; as a result, clashes often occurred between the islanders and the foreigners. In these battles, the Okinawans were forced to use primitive weapons or their bare hands and feet.

Painfully aware of their lack of success in the skirmishes, the various Okinawan ch'uan fa and tode groups united. A new fighting style was thus formed, combining the *open hands* and *feet* of the ch'uan fa and the *fists* of the tode system. The new type of unarmed combat became known as "te," which means hand. This is the first known record of the art of karate in a nearly modern form. Unfortunately, little more of its early development is written. Since Te practitioners were forced underground to escape detection from the Satsuma samurai, most of the early history is based upon oral tradition.

Japan

Japan, like other countries of the East, is reputed to have had a type of unarmed fighting very early in its history. The earliest style probably resembled a type of desperate wrestling more than anything else. According to the *Koji-Ki*, an ancient chronicle of Japan, the first true Japanese combative art, jujitsu, burst upon the scene around 23 B.C. A wrestler named Tomakesu-Hayato was considered to be the most effective battler of the age. He was arrogant and insolent about his combative abilities, but when he fought a match with Nomi-no-Sukune, by order of the emperor, he was defeated and kicked to death. Nomi-no-Sukune is considered to be the founder of jujitsu.

In A.D. 607, the earliest recorded cultural exchange took place between Japan and China. Shortly after, there was a great Chinese influx into Japan. Undoubtedly, they brought some forms of the art of ch'uan fa with them. Apparently the introduction of Chinese methods was assimilated into the jujitsu art since there are again many similarities between the two styles.

In 1917, an Okinawan language professor, Gichin Funakoshi, was invited to Japan to demonstrate the Okinawan-te techniques. His demonstration so impressed the Japanese that he was flooded with requests to remain and teach in Tokyo. As might be expected, the Okinawan style was modified by the jujitsu art as well as by the Korean style of karate that was also being introduced into Japan at about the same time. The Japanese called their new fighting art "karate" (kara = empty, te = hand). Actually the term is something of a misnomer, since the feet are used as well as the hands.

Korea

Tae Kwon Do is the Korean term for a system of unarmed combat that today is nearly identical to Japanese karate. The origins of Tae Kwon Do, however, can be traced to ancient Korean history.

As stated previously, an Indian Buddhist monk introduced an early form of karate into China. The monks at the Shaolin Monastery were the first to become proficient in the art and in turn taught it to other monks. Traveling throughout the far corners of the Orient preaching Buddhism, the monks also spread the knowledge of ch'uan fa (Chinese Kempo Boxing). Usually it was integrated into the already existing forms of local unarmed combat. Ch'uan fa was thus introduced into the northern provinces of Korea during the fourth century and evolved into the early form of Tae Kwon Do called Tae Kyon.

Typically, the art at first flourished only on temple grounds with the spiritual aspects intricately entwined with the physical techniques. Later, in the seventh century, the skills were passed on to, and eagerly accepted by, the general populace for self-protection. The times were especially violent due to the intense quarreling and outbursts of fighting between the three kingdoms that comprised the area presently known as Korea.

After a prolonged struggle, the kingdom of Silla emerged victorious, and in A.D. 668 the kingdoms were unified under a central government. The Silla period lasted until A.D. 935 and was considered the golden age in Korea's history. It was a time of building and creativity. Two stone sculptures depicting karatelike techniques, the forerunners of present-day forms, still exist. These statues, which date to the mid-eighth century, stood guard at the entrance to a temple housing a huge stone Buddha. Their presence suggests a close association between religion and Tae Kwon Do as it existed at the time.

Also during the early Silla period, another group sprang up which proved to be as important to the growth of Tae Kwon Do in Korea as were the Buddhist monks. They called themselves the Hwa-Rang-Do, and their purpose was to cultivate moral and patriotic ideals among Korean youth. Membership in this exclusive organization was restricted to educated young men of noble birth. The members led an existence which was conducive to moral improvement as they traveled throughout the country training their bodies and spirits. Tenets of their moral code, which resembled that of the European knights or the samurai of Japan, were as follows:

1. loyalty to the king,
2. faithfulness to one's friends,
3. devotion to one's parents,
4. bravery and absolute obedience on the battlefield,
5. a prohibition against wanton killing of any form of life.

There was a natural affinity between the principles of Hwa-Rang-Do and those of the Tae Kyon. Before long, the latter became part of the official training of the Hwa-Rang-Do and contributed much to its character. The eventual wedding of the two groups resulted in a martial art which, according to Western standards, has a paradoxical basis of magnanimity, sympathy, and love (respect for the worth of one's opponent). This kind of emotional foundation exists in all forms of karate, but continues to be particularly strong in the modern Korean style (Tae Kwon Do).

The greatest era in the history of Tae Kyon, ironically, came after the end of Korea's golden era. In A.D. 935, the kingdom of Silla was overthrown by the warlord Kyonghum who then established the kingdom of Koryo from which the Western name of Korea was derived. Founded as it was by a warlord, Koryo remained strongly martial in spirit. During this period some of the nation's finest soldiers were produced who time after time successfully defended their homeland against invaders. Being dedicated students of Tae Kyon, the men sometimes trained by slamming their fists into walls or blocks of wood in order to strengthen their hands. This practice is still performed by many devotees of karate.

Inevitably, the Koryo dynasty declined after five hundred years of rule, and the practice of Tae Kyon declined as well. In the fifteenth century the era of the warrior princes ended and was replaced by the Yi dynasty, which held learning and scholarship in highest esteem. Confucianism replaced Buddhism as the state religion and the military arts fell into disrepute. For four centuries, the political fortunes of Korea declined along with its interest in Tae Kyon. The final blow came in 1910 when the Japanese overran Korea. Tae Kyon was barely alive at the time.

Bent on destroying the national identity of the Koreans in the hope that it would then be replaced by loyalty to them, the Japanese banned the practice of Tae Kyon. Their orders were generally obeyed. Only in the remote rural areas did the practice of Tae Kyon continue. The order, however, was not as detrimental to the development of Tae Kwon Do as one might expect. Finding their life oppressive at home, many Koreans left to study and work in China and Japan, where there were no restrictions on the practice of martial arts. As a result, for the first time in over a thousand years, the practitioners of Tae Kyon were exposed to other forms of karate.

The end of World War II brought an end to Japan's thirty-six year occupation of Korea. It also brought home thousands of Koreans who were fired by intense feelings of patriotism and national pride. As part of the national movement to restore Korean traditions, interest in self-defense methods was revived and many experts opened dojangs (karate schools). They returned from all parts of the Orient, bringing with them many new techniques gleaned from Chinese Kempo, and Okinawan and Japanese karate. Wisely, they proceeded to blend the various new and old styles into the modern Korean system practiced today.

The leaders of the dojangs decided to search for a new and more meaningful name for the Korean art of self-defense. Finally, in 1955, the term *Tae Kwon Do* was adopted by the leading masters of the art. Suggested by Choi Hong Hi, this name accurately describes the techniques of this self-defense method. Translated, "Tae" means to kick or smash with the feet; "Kwon" refers to punching with the fists; and "Do" is the art of destroying with the fists and feet.

This choice proved wise for two reasons. First, it sounds very much like the ancient term "Tae Kyon," which provided an historical continuity and helped the Koreans bolster their national pride. Second, the name is descriptive of both hand and foot techniques, thus being a more accurate term than karate which refers solely to the hands. Still, Japanese karate and Korean Tae Kwon Do are nearly identical systems of self-defense.

The United States

The art of karate was practically unknown in the United States until after the Second World War. Significant growth of the activity in this country did not occur until the Korean War (1948–1951). During and after this conflict many American soldiers were exposed to karate while stationed in Japan and Korea. Some even joined training schools and became rather proficient. The chief impetus in the United States, however, was provided by karate master Matsutatsu Oyama in 1952 when he gave a series of demonstrations throughout the United States.

Oyama limited his demonstrations primarily to a variety of karate routines called *kata*. These consist of intricate but predetermined series of blocks, punches, and kicks that one executes against an imaginary opponent or opponents (see Chapter 7, for an example). This is the traditional method of training since karate is so lethal a fighting form that actual competition would very likely result in the death or serious injury of one of the participants. American audiences who were not accustomed to such training found the "choreography" difficult to understand and sometimes even amusing. They did, however, applaud when Oyama demonstrated the breaking of boards and bricks with his bare hands. Although such techniques are only a very small part of karate training in the Orient, the audiences placed undue emphasis on the board-breaking demonstrations. The recent surge in American participation in karate is leading to a more accurate view of the physical aspects of the art.

It is most distressing that the spiritual aspect of karate tends to be neglected in the United States and in other Western countries. Part of the reason, paradoxically, may be the traditional relationship existing between karate and the Buddhist religion. Many Occidentals feel they cannot possibly comprehend or achieve the proper spiritual levels because they are not Buddhists. Consequently, they do not attempt to understand the spiritual basis or even ignore it completely. One must keep in mind that it is not necessary to be a Buddhist, or belong to any religion for that matter, to be spiritually guided in an activity like karate. What is important to avoid unnecessary violence is to allow oneself to be guided by his love for others. Love is defined here as having a feeling of respect for others, treating others with compassion or at least with tolerance, and acting courteously and patiently toward them.

It must also be remembered that Orientals have for many centuries been taught the relationship between the acquisition of martial arts and the responsibility for using such skills maturely, in a spiritualistic manner. This concept, while not completely foreign to Western cultures, has not generally received as great an emphasis here as it has in the East. Hopefully, this condition will change with the widespread infusion of karate into the Western world.

Much of the spiritual neglect in karate can be placed at the feet of poorly qualified instructors. These people usually lack a thorough knowledge of the historical background of the art and an understanding of the spiritual basis of karate. There can be little wonder then that they fail to instill the proper attitudes in their students. Instructors must stress that karate skills should never be used offensively or to "showoff." Indeed, when one has acquired the means of effective self-defense, one generally has also developed enough self-confidence that the *need* to prove oneself no longer exists. Of course, a certain amount of maturity is required to conduct oneself responsibly and with restraint.

If a student does not demonstrate desirable personality traits, the instructor is duty-bound to withhold advanced training until that student is socially and spiritually ready. Giving an immature person the capability of critically or fatally injuring another is akin to putting a loaded gun in the hands of a child. The child is less to blame, if damage is done, than the person who provided the gun. In a similar way, instructors should consider themselves responsible for their students' actions. While it is true that instructors are not infallible in evaluating their students' personalities, they must always give careful consideration before allowing anyone to progress to more advanced levels.

The impression thus far may suggest that karate in the United States is in a sad state. Nothing could be farther from the truth. The United States has been the "melting pot" of the world in many ways, including the evolution of the martial arts. Because of a lack of tradition in karate, Americans have not felt as fervently bound to a particular style as Orientals have historically been. True, the first instructors in the United States were Orientals and many still are. But while each teacher represented a specific system, the students had the opportunity to try many styles and decide for themselves which was most effective. Due to their democratic background, individual American students also tend to feel free to "bend" traditional techniques to conform to their own physiques and personalities.

American karate is rapidly becoming recognized as a unique style. It is still in its infancy and is continuing to develop, but it is already being characterized as creative, individualistic, exciting, and quite effective as a combative art. In fact, there are indications that Oriental karate associations are somewhat reluctant to enter international tournaments in the United States for fear of being beaten and "losing face."

KARATE AS A SPORT

In addition to being pragmatic (if it works, use it), Americans have a competitive nature. It is not surprising then to find that the most recent innovations in karate originated in the United States. For the first time karate has become a *sport* with rules and regulations guiding its conduct. This additional dimension has made the activity more appealing to large numbers of participants.

International competition, though, faces several obstacles which severely limit continued growth of the sport. If they are not solved, karate will never achieve its potential as a major international sport. The chief problem is that there are more than forty different styles of karate around the world and the resulting lack of standardization of rules often makes it very difficult for adherents of different styles to compete fairly against each other. Judging is difficult enough even when competitors are trained in the same school.

Unfortunately, standardization of rules and conduct appears unlikely since karate practitioners are usually intensely devoted to their styles. Each firmly believes his method is superior to all others. Understandably, they are quite resistant to change. This impasse can only be surmounted by the leaders of the most popular styles devising and agreeing to a standardized form of karate. That they will do so in the near future is almost inconceivable, though it would be a milestone in the history of the sport.

Another problem that competition presents concerns protective equipment and the force with which blows are allowed to land. Obviously, when safety equipment is not permitted in competition, the blows must be carefully controlled to reduce the chance of injury. Many people feel that the checking of blows at the point of contact, results in the development of undesirable habits that carry over in actual combat. This would, of course, defeat the self-defense purposes for which karate is well respected.

When protective equipment is required, more forceful blows are permitted in competition. Unfortunately, such equipment restricts the participants in their speed and range of motion, and creates an artificial situation. At any rate, the controversy has yet to be settled. Perhaps the "middle road" is the answer with skillfully designed costumes that offer more protection while allowing normal mobility providing a compromise.

Amateur competition will almost assuredly remain a controlled contact sport. In 1975, *professional* competition was inaugurated. At this level, full contact is the rule since it is more appealing to spectators. Still, competitors are required to wear especially designed safety pads on their hands and feet, as shown in Fig. 1-1.

The hurdles obstructing the international standardization of competition presently seem insurmountable. Yet the sport is still young and the required measures are unmistakably clear. One can only conclude, optimistically, that the leaders will take the unselfish and mature steps necessary to encourage the continued worldwide growth of karate. Surely, a belief in the potential physical and spiritual benefits to mankind should far outweigh any personal reluctance to change.

Fig. 1-1.
Safety equipment for hands and feet. The "Stars and Stripes" gi worn by Bill Wallace is made exclusively for the United States Professional Karate Team.

2 UNIFORM, EQUIPMENT, AND CLASS PROCEDURES

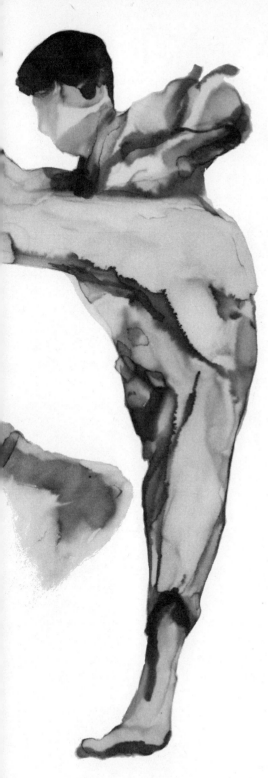

No special uniform or equipment is *absolutely* necessary for karate training. Various instructional aids, however, are very helpful and should be used if they can be acquired.

UNIFORM

Gi

The *gi* is the name of the pajamalike uniform traditionally worn by those engaged in karate. Even more than a uniform, though, it is an instructional aid. If any object should be required, it is the gi. By wearing a gi, beginners immediately start to think of themselves as karatekas (karate players). Such a psychological framework or "set" allows one to move in a less inhibited manner. Thus freed of inhibitions, one is able to devote more attention and energy to learning karate skills. The adverse effect of inhibitions upon skillful and graceful movement is seen in all athletic endeavors from dancing to boxing, but is particularly apparent in karate where the movement forms are foreign to most people.

When the gi and athletic supporter are worn during practice, no other articles are necessary. Indeed, shoes, bracelets, rings, and necklaces are forbidden for safety purposes. Fingernails and toenails should be kept short and clean for the same reasons.

The karate gi usually comes in seven sizes. So as not to restrict movement, they must be loose fitting. The following list should help the beginning student determine the most suitable size for his or her height.

Size	Measurements		Jacket length	Pants length	Belt length
0	For children		28″	26½″	77″
1	Under 4'9″	Less than 105 lbs.	30½″	29″	79½″
2	4'10″–5'3″	106–120	36″	31½″	88″
3	5'4″–5'6″	121–135	38″	34″	95½″
4	5'7″–5'9″	136–165	39½″	37½″	102″
5	5'10″–6'	166–200	40″	39″	111″
6	6'1″	200 & over	50½″	41½″	120″

White is the traditional color of the gi, although black is occasionally seen. Although there is actually no rule against wearing any color gi, variation is not encouraged. Because of this, many feel it is discouraged, and it is to some extent. Some feel this attitude is unfortunate since colorful uniforms can contribute much to player and team morale, and to spectator appeal, besides allowing for individual expression. Consider, for instance, the racing silks of jockeys, or the bright hues of basketball and football uniforms, and even boxing trunks. Karate suits *are* available with colored trim; however, when a gi of this type is worn the color of the trim must correspond to the belt color.

Belts

Perhaps the best reason for wearing a white uniform is that it allows the color of the belt to stand out distinctly. Unlike gi color, the color of the belt is extremely significant, since it represents the level of proficiency one has attained in karate. One might expect each of the twenty possible ranks to be assigned a different color belt, but that is not always the case. In Japan, for instance, only three colors are used: white for beginners, brown for intermediate ranks, and black for the advanced karateka. Many more colors are employed in Europe; sometimes a color is assigned for each rank. This practice is apparently felt to be desirable from the standpoint of achievement, recognition, player motivation, and spectator appeal. In the United States a middle course is usually followed. Yet, there is still considerable variation regarding belt colors.

The chart (opposite) lists the belt colors most often used in karate in the United States. Included are the Japanese and Korean names for each rank. The lower ten (kyu) grades include all the ranks up to the black-belt level. The upper division includes the ten black-belt (dan) degrees.

Not only are there variations in the belt color assigned for each rank, but the requirements also vary with each system. However, there are many similarities. As the karateka progresses, each succeeding degree becomes more difficult to achieve and takes longer to acquire. Criteria for promotion include such things as attendance and participation in recognized classes, a knowledge of karate history and philosophy, exhibition of stances and techniques, demonstration of one or more kata, prearranged sparring, free-style sparring, and participation in competitive tournaments. Not all of these criteria are included in every examination, however. In addition to meeting the physical and intellectual standards, one must display to the satisfaction of his teacher such attitudes as gentleness, humility, and responsibility. Advancement to the fifth-degree black belt, and those beyond, is generally awarded not on the basis of formal tests, but on one's contribution to the field of karate. Examples include the addition of new knowledge, the development of recognized kata, and the promotion of the art.

Grade	Color of belt	Japanese names	Korean names
10	white	Ju Kyu	Sip Gup
9	white	Ku Kyu	Koo Gup
8	yellow	Hachi Kyu	Pal Gup
7	green	Shichi Kyu	Chil Gup
6	green	Rok Kyu	Yook Gup
5	blue	Go Kyu	Oh Gup
4	purple	Yon Kyu	Sa Gup
3	brown	San Kyu	Sam Gup
2	brown	Ni Kyu	Yi Gup
1	brown	Ik Kyu	Il Gup

Degree	Color of belt	Japanese names	Korean names
1	black	Shodan	Chodan
2	black	Nidan	Yidan
3	black	Sandan	Samdan
4	black	Yodan	Sadan
5	black	Godan	Ohdan
6	black	Rokudan	Yook Dan
7	black	Shichidan	Chil Dan
8	black	Hachidan	Pal Dan
9	black	Dudan	Koo Dan
10	black	Judan	Sip Dan

procedure for tying the belt

The belt is tied in a square knot. For those not acquainted with knot tying, Fig. 2-1 will clarify the procedure. First, tie the jacket securely (B, C). After folding the belt in half to determine the center (D), place the centerpoint at the front of the waist (E). Then carry each end around the back (F) and continue to the front (G), and there tie the knot. From (G), draw the overlapping end of the belt up between the jacket and the belt (H) and complete the knot as shown (I–K). It is considered a matter of pride for the ends of the belt to be of equal length after the square knot is neatly tied (K, L).

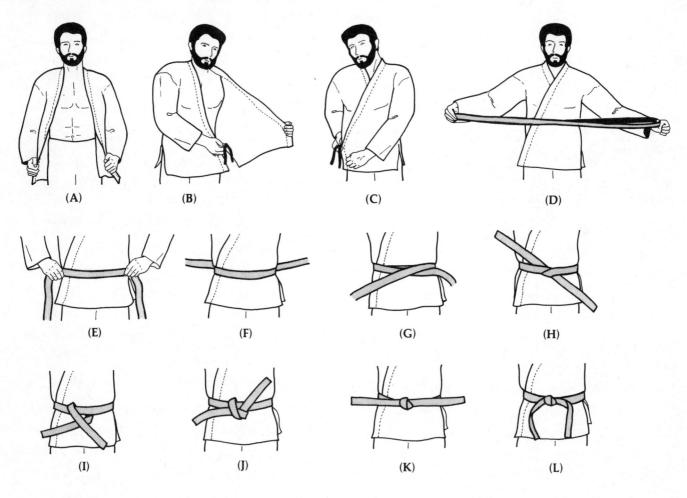

(A)   (B)   (C)   (D)

(E)   (F)   (G)   (H)

(I)   (J)   (K)   (L)

Fig. 2-1.
Procedure for tying the karate belt

EQUIPMENT

Full-length Mirror

A full-length mirror is probably the most basic and useful piece of equipment a karateka can have because it helps to check his or her form. It is particularly convenient if an instructor is not available, or in large classes where the instructor does not have a lot of time to devote to each student. Often, students will believe that they are executing their movements correctly, even when told otherwise. A mirror, of course, provides the student with visual proof of flaws. Once convinced of an error a student is, of course, more motivated to correct it.

While not everyone has a full-length mirror, many schools and colleges do have a specially designed room for dance instruction. These rooms almost invariably have mirrors along the walls for self-evaluation of one's skills. Similarly, a small community may have a private dance school but not one of karate. A group of karate enthusiasts will usually be able to reserve a mirrored room for a few hours each day or week, for a small fee.

A video tape recorder, though quite expensive, is even more valuable than a mirror. It allow's one's performance to be recorded and then replayed for evaluation comparison. Again, many schools have such machines, especially in their physical education departments.

Striking Devices

After becoming relatively proficient at delivering a variety of karate techniques, one should begin practicing against a target that provides some resistance upon contact. Besides the strength-building benefits, the resistance offers better preparation in terms of actual combat. Even though one may be engaged in karate for exercise benefits and may never intend to use karate skills in a combative situation, the occasion may very well arise whereby self-defense becomes mandatory. If a combatant is not accustomed to the feeling of forceful contact, the effectiveness of his or her blocks and blows will be considerably reduced.

Certainly a karateka cannot use human beings as targets for powerful techniques unless protective clothing is worn. It is simpler and safer to practice against inanimate targets, a variety of which are shown and discussed in this section.

makiwara

A makiwara is the traditional object that is used by an aspiring karateka in training. Basically, it is an upright post with a padded target area for striking. Makiwara are available commercially, but it is not difficult to construct one. Fig. 2-2 (A) shows the simplest type. A seven-foot length of 2" x 4" lumber can be used for the post, although a 4" x 4" piece is better. If the latter is used, it *must* be beveled so that the thickness is about one half-inch at the top and about three inches at the bottom. This gives the post the necessary flexibility or "give."

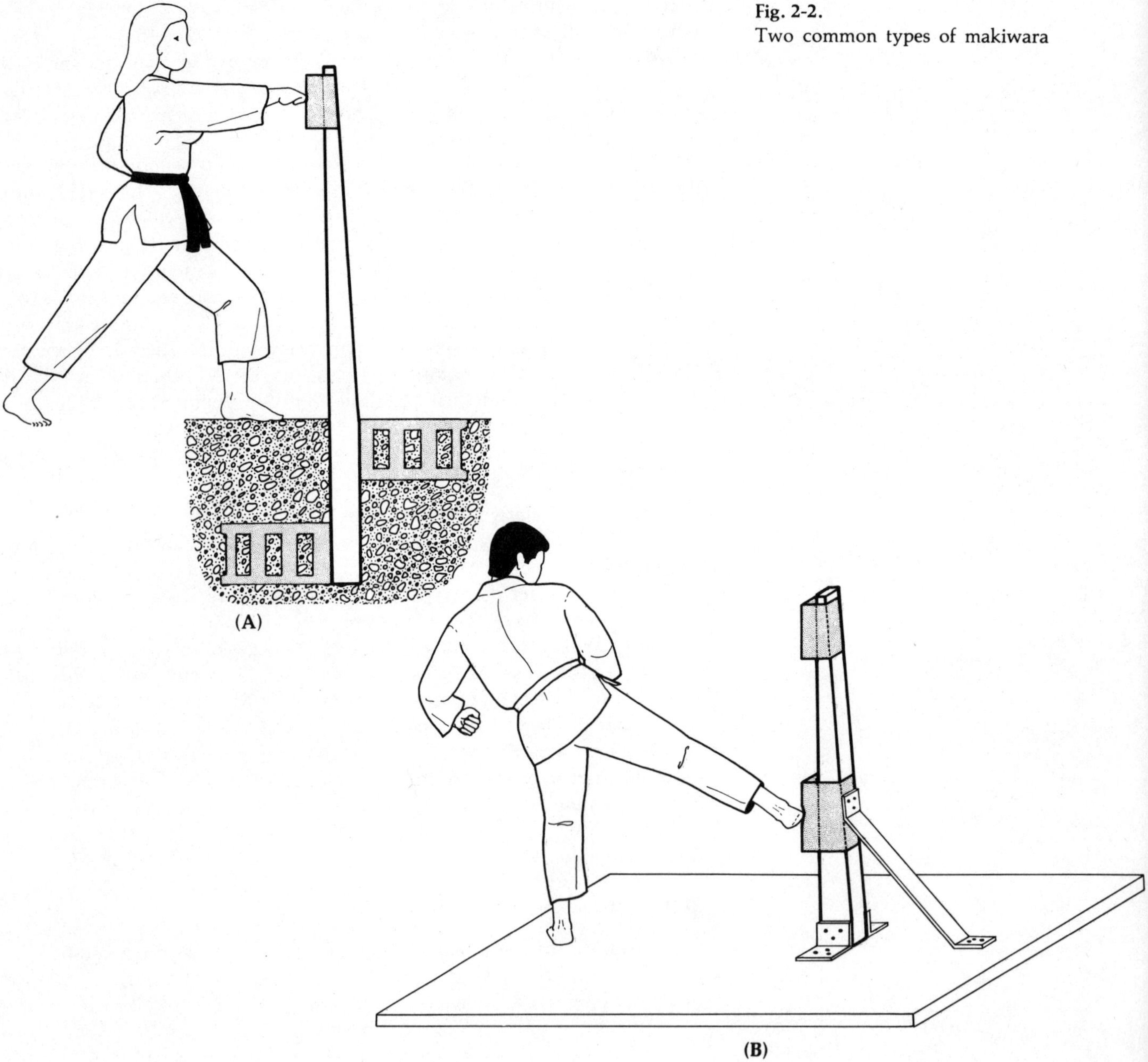

Fig. 2-2.
Two common types of makiwara

(A)

(B)

The striking target can be made of an eight-inch length of sponge rubber covered with, and attached to the post by, canvas. Depending upon individual preferences, the thickness of the rubber may range from two to four inches. If thick foam rubber is used, a one-inch pad may even be suitable.

The post is sunk far enough into the ground that the midpoint of the striking pad is at the level of one's solar plexus (see Fig. 2-2). Notice the post is not perfectly perpendicular but leans slightly toward the karateka. To help stabilize the post, concrete blocks are braced against it before the post-hole is refilled.

Figure 2-2(B) shows a portable makiwara. It requires more effort to construct but is more practical. The braces at the sides and rear are made of metal. In this model an additional striking pad has been attached to the post so a greater variety of blows may be practiced.

training bag

A training bag is a heavy cylinder-shaped bag that is attached to a ceiling, and is traditionally used by boxers. Unfortunately, those bags designed for boxing do not usually wear well since they are not built to withstand the rigors of concentrated blows, especially kicks. Recently, however, more durable models have been constructed specifically for karate use and are now appearing on the market.

A karateka can use the training bag without assistance. Often, though, a training partner will hold it as shown in Fig. 2-3 to increase the resistance offered by the bag.

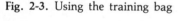

Fig. 2-3. Using the training bag

blocking dummies and punching mitts

One can usually obtain a football blocking dummy (Fig. 2-4A) or a push-back dummy (B) from a football team or a sporting goods store. One drawback is that a partner is absolutely necessary to hold these kinds of targets for the karateka. On the other hand, they have all the other advantages of a regular training bag and are much less expensive. In addition, the person holding a dummy can move about rapidly and offer a moving target, because it is not attached to anything and is relatively light. Punching mitts (C) are used in a very similar way to the dummies. Before long the person holding these target devices will be trying to outwit the karateka and make him or her miss the target. Of all the training aids, these are the most fun to use.

Fig. 2-4.
Blocking dummies and punching mitt

(A) (B) (C)

punching ball

This device consists of an inflatable ball that is attached to the ceiling and floor with elastic cords (Fig. 2-5). Because it is light, it does not afford much resistance to punches, so it is not a strength developer. On the other hand, since the ball moves about quite rapidly, the student is given ample opportunity to develop his reflexes and muscular speed. For the most benefit, a karateka should use the ball as a sparring partner; that is, while moving about in all directions, he or she should deliver a variety of techniques based upon split-second decisions.

The light pear-shaped striking bag that is attached by a swivel connection to a rebound platform (Fig. 2-6) can also be used for practicing karate

Fig. 2-5. Punching ball

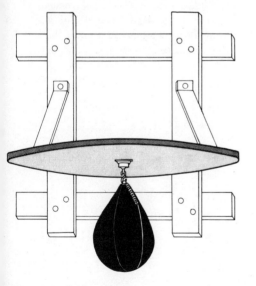

Fig. 2-6. Striking bag

punches and kicks. It is not as practical as a punching ball, however, *for karate*.

Sparring (mock fighting) is excellent training for combat, but it cannot be employed until students have developed nearly perfect control of their techniques. Karatekas in the beginning stages of training do not possess this skill. Nor can it be assumed that they have the psychological control to restrain themselves from harming another during the excitement of sparring matches. Only an experienced teacher of karate is qualified to make accurate appraisals of student readiness, both physical and emotional. Chapter six is devoted to sparring and to the use of karate in self-defense.

CLASS PROCEDURES

General Considerations

A karate class must reflect the spiritual qualities upon which the martial art is historically and philosophically founded. Even the training area should help set the tone. Traditionally, a spacious but simple and immaculate environment assists in creating an atmosphere of dignity and sincerity for training.

More relevant than physical surroundings, of course, are the attitudes existing between students, between student and instructor, and toward the use of karate in general. Therefore in addition to the development of physical skills, the conduct of a karate class must be such that it helps instill spiritual attitudes and behavior in students.

Discipline is the fundamental attitude, and is the most prominent characteristic observed in viewing a class. For example, except for sparring sessions, the entire class performs their workout in unison. Also, except for the instructor's voice and the sounds of movement and effort, silence prevails. Besides showing respect for the teacher who is trying to impart knowledge and understanding, the silence reflects consideration of one's fellow students who are attempting to learn. Time is set aside, naturally, for the instructor to answer students' questions. Punctuality is demanded for the same reasons as silence. A student who is habitually tardy should not be permitted to continue practicing in the class because of this disruptive influence. An instructor who allows such inconsideration and disrespect is remiss in his duty.

Not only is discipline demanded during class, but excessively loud talking and rough-housing in the training area before and after class are also prohibited. Such activities are the antithesis of gentleness, courtesy and control. Besides, employing karate skills indiscriminately in such rough-housing may lead to injuries or create ill feelings. Maturity is obviously required if one is to limit the use of martial arts to controlled practice, competition, or self-defense. However, maturity is not acquired overnight. By constantly stressing control in the training area, it is hoped that eventually self-control will develop and carry over into every facet of one's life.

Lining Up

A class generally begins with the command, "Line up," although in some schools the sounding of a bell or gong signifies the beginning. In any case, a class forms ranks according to the diagram in Fig. 2-7. Each triangle represents a karateka and an arrow indicates the direction each faces. The instructor is represented by an encircled triangle. If only a few *dans* (black belters) are present, they usually line up adjacent to the instructor and face the *kyus* (students who have not yet earned black belts). Lowest ranking dans should station themselves next to the instructor while higher ranking ones should be situated progressively further from him. In the diagram, the number under each triangle indicates the relative rank of each person with the instructor being number one.

The highest ranking kyus will be stationed on the righthand side of the first line (positions 5, 6, and 7). Progressively lower ranking persons will line up next to them (positions 8, 9, and 10). If there are a large number of high ranking kyus, they will fill positions in the second row starting on the right side (position 11). White belt karatekas will comprise the remainder of the positions (12-28). If there are only a few high ranking kyus, white belters will also be in the first row.

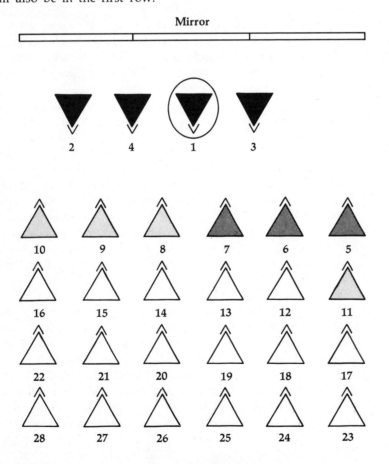

Fig. 2-7.
Proper positioning for lining up in a karate class. Black triangles represent dans (black belters). The other triangles stand for kyus—the darkest shades indicating the most advanced degrees, the white triangles representing the white belters.

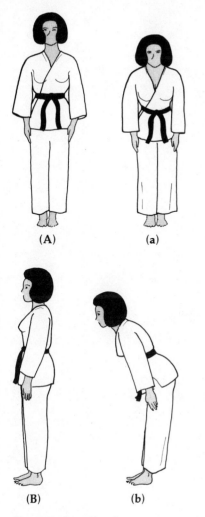

(A)   (a)

(B)   (b)

Fig. 2-8. Standing bow

Bowing

Students usually line up in the attention stance (Fig. 2-8 A). Some schools, though, require the more traditional and formal kneeling position (Fig. 2-9 A). After the class has lined up in the preferred position, the teacher will issue the command, "Attention," and then about a second later, "Bow." Upon this signal, both students and instructor will bow as indicated in Figs. 2-8 (a, b) or 2-9 (a, b). They hesitate at the bowed position for about a second before returning, upon command, to the starting stance (A, B).

During the kneeling bow, the karetekas' eyes are directed toward the floor. With the more informal standing bow, however, the students' eyes are directed toward the instructor at chest level. For the students the bow is a token of respect for the teacher. Traditionally, though, the teacher always bows a bit lower than the students. In addition to showing them respect, this gesture symbolizes his humility. Unfortunately, in the Western world this token of humility is not always reflective of the instructor's true attitude. If the instructor does not reveal gentle, humble, and disciplined behavior, it is not likely that the students will acquire them either since the most effective teaching is by example.

At the end of each training session, the class again lines up and goes through the bowing ceremony before being dismissed by the instructor.

Class Activities

After the bowing-in, everyone again assumes the attention stance (Fig. 2-8A), and the instructor leads the class in the warming-up and stretching exercises prescribed in Chapter 3. Following this, the class works on basic techniques which include blocks, punches, and kicks. There is no definite plan for this activity. Much is left to the individual teacher's discretion and philosophy. Some begin with blocking movement while others begin with punches or kicks. Usually, previously learned skills are reviewed and practiced first, then new techniques are introduced. The entire class practices simultaneously, if space allows.

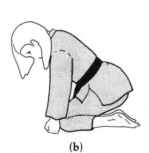

(A)   (a)   (B)   (b)   **Fig. 2-9.** Kneeling bow

An instructor will generally face the students while they are practicing and also perform the techniques so they have a model to emulate. By facing them, he is also able to observe their mistakes and take steps to correct them. Sometimes an instructor will face the same direction the students are facing and lead them "follow the leader" style. This method is often used when the class moves across the floor in a series of stances from which techniques are executed.

There is no single best way to teach karate skills, just as there is no best way to teach English or mathematics. Each teacher has found what works best for him based on his philosophy and personality. Also, different methods work for different students. Thus it is against all principles of professional education to expect conformity. Most teachers recognize this and try to devote part of each period to individual evaluation and instruction. However, in large classes this becomes difficult.

In spite of the great variety in teaching styles, one can expect every instructor to cover the material presented in this book.

Meditation

Occasionally, an instructor will provide time for meditation at the beginning of each class, just after the bowing-in ritual. Every teacher *should* provide this time, if only because the remainder of the workout will progress more efficiently. Typically, the meditation period will last about five minutes (longer if time permits). It helps to clear the mind of all irrelevant thoughts so one can devote his entire mental processes to learning karate. Most people do not realize how difficult or how important it is to acquire the ability to meditate successfully. Eliminating outside irrelevancies helps one to concentrate on *any* subject. As a result one is better able to deal with them.

Through practice, the ability to focus thoughts readily and easily can be developed. The beginner will normally need assistance. With the class in the position normally assumed for meditation (Fig. 2-10), the teacher will

Fig. 2-10.
Kneeling position for meditation

choose an object such as a statue, animal, or plant and ask the students to close their eyes and visualize the object and try to eliminate all *other* visions and thoughts from their minds. As with other aspects of karate, meditation depends upon discipline and control. Ideally, these characteristics will be limited not merely to karate involvement, but will eventually become deeply ingrained facets of one's personality.

After a few sessions the teacher will encourage students to choose their own subjects for meditation. The ability to focus one's mental energies is useful not only throughout the entire practice period but throughout life. One should try to concentrate completely during every phase of his work-out, including the warm-up, technique drills, and kata performance. The student will be pleased to discover that meditation and the subsequent deep concentration during the karate session will leave his mind relaxed, refreshed, and free of emotional turmoil even after the karate class has ended.

3 WARMING UP AND STRETCHING ACTIVITIES

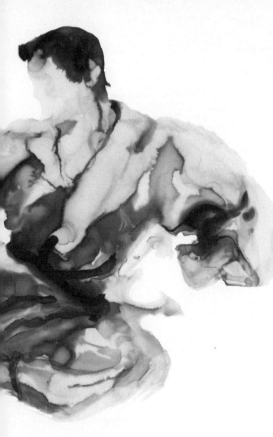

GENERAL INFORMATION

The degree to which a skilled craftsman can achieve his or her goals depends in large measure upon available tools. Athletes' chief tools are their bodies. They *must* know how to prepare them for activity. Proper preparation includes a warm-up and stretching period. This should precede *each* athletic training session. This period is especially important for karate training because flexibility is a basic requirement for successful performance in most karate skills.

Warm-up

The term *warm-up* is accurately descriptive. It refers to the fact that the temperature of the body, including the muscles and blood, actually does increase during physical activity. To be beneficial, however, the temperature increase must be sufficient to result in certain necessary physiological changes. As a rule of thumb, one may accept light sweating as indication of an adequate warm-up.

Increased muscle and blood temperatures permit (1) an increase in both *speed* and *strength* of muscular contractions and (2) an increase in the rate at which *oxygen* can be delivered to and utilized by active muscles. These factors, along with others, result in an increase in speed, strength, coordination, efficiency, and endurance. One's athletic performance will, obviously, thereby be improved through a proper warm-up. Even more significant, an adequate warm-up is beneficial in helping to prevent muscle soreness and injury.

There are many ways in which an athlete can warm up. *Passive* methods include heating by hot baths, hot showers, steam and sauna rooms, and diathermy. These procedures have gained but few followers, perhaps due to their limitations regarding availability of facilities.

As the name implies, *active* warm-up methods involve muscular effort by the athlete. Procedures may be divided into two categories, unrelated (general) and related methods. A general mobilization of the body can be brought about by calesthenic exercises and can result in the desired physiological changes.

Related methods employ the same skills that are to be used later in the training session or in competition. In addition to the practice effect, it has all the physiological benefits of the unrelated procedures.

Stretching

Stretching exercises should be stressed during the warm-up period. These are beneficial in increasing one's flexibility—the range of movement in the joints of the body. Good flexibility makes it possible to have proper alignment of the body which is necessary for graceful, efficient movement. Figure 5-32 shows an excellent example of the necessity for extraordinary flexibility in the karate participant. Most important, flexibility exercises during the warm-up period help to prevent *injury* to the muscles and tendons during the practice session or competition.

Surprisingly, with stretching activities one is not concerned primarily with stretching one's muscles, as is generally believed, but with stretching the associated connective tissue. This includes the fascia that surrounds muscle fibers, and the tendons by which the muscles are attached to bones. The term, *muscle stretching*, is very common and there is nothing wrong with using it as long as one is aware of the true meaning.

Connective tissue may be stretched either by employing bouncing (phasic) motions, or by very slow (static) motions. Phasic movements, though utilized most often by athletes, are not as beneficial as static movements. While tendons and fascia are effectively stretched by both kinds of motions, phasic movements are not as easily controlled and may exceed the limits intended at that time. In addition, a muscle that is stretched with jerky motions reacts by contracting (shortening) reflexly. The contractions are, of course, diametrically opposed to the desired stretching action. Further, as the bouncing movements intensify in range or speed, the tension in the muscles increases. Besides interfering with the stretching of tendons and fascia, the additional tension increases the likelihood of injury to the muscles.

Static stretching methods which are based on sounder physiological principles are, unfortunately, seldom employed by athletes. Very slow and deliberate stretching movements actually *inhibit contraction* in the muscles being stretched. Therefore, the tension in the muscles *decreases* even though the surrounding and associated connective tissue is being stretched. Research shows that, for a given degree of stretch, the amount of tension produced in muscles by a jerky motion is more than twice that of a slow stretch. The latter is, therefore, much less likely to cause muscular soreness or injury. When employing the static procedures, a stretched position should be held for at least one minute for optimal increases in flexibility.

To increase the range of motion in a joint it is necessary to push beyond the usual range. Thus, some degree of discomfort *should* be experienced. One must be careful, however, not to stretch so far as to cause injury. After stretching a muscle group it usually feels good to relax the muscles and shake them rather vigorously.

In warming up and stretching, the instructor must be prepared to allow for individual preferences, especially in the case of the experienced athlete. An enforced and complete departure from his usual warm-up procedures may psychologically hinder such a person in performing at his best. However, it does behoove *every* athlete to seriously consider the preceding suggestions which are based upon sound physiological factors.

Besides the psychological variations, there are many physical differences among individuals. One person, for example, may be "tight" in the shoulder region but "loose" and flexible in the lumbar (lower back) region. Another person may be just the opposite. Because of the individual physical differences, it is impossible to devise a *specific* warming-up and stretching routine that will be of optimum benefit to all. Presented below, however, is a general warm-up program that may be followed prior to karate competition or, with slight modification, a practice session.

1. Stretching Movements—At first, employ very slow movements with special attention to those joints that require extra stretching. If the athlete feels phasic stretching motions must be included, they should follow the static ones.

2. General Activity Exercises—Involve the large muscle groups and continue to the point of light sweating.

3. Related Activity Exercises
   a) Practice specific karate techniques, e.g., punches, kicks, and blocks.
   b) More advanced karate players should practice a kata (see Chapter 7). Stop warming up about 10 minutes before sparring or competition is to begin.

4. Light Sporadic Movements—This is basically a rest period during which the athlete delivers an occasional punch or kick at an imaginary opponent. A few stretching or exercise movements should also be included to maintain the warmed-up condition.

This warm-up may be a bit too strenuous for the beginning karateka. If so, this indicates that he or she has not yet reached a satisfactory level of physical fitness.

A thorough, but not exhausting, warm-up is extremely important. It has been wisely stated that, "If the warm-up is right, the performance is a cinch—it's all downhill."

SPECIFIC WARMING-UP AND STRETCHING EXERCISES

The remainder of this chapter is devoted to the presentation of specific warming-up and stretching exercises.

Usually, one begins by exercising the neck muscles and works down to the ankles. In this way all of the body parts are warmed up and stretched. Each exercise should begin with slow stretching movements, with the range of motion being small at first and then increasing. The exercises should also be performed with increasing vigor to achieve a warmed-up condition. How rapidly one progresses from slow to vigorous movements depends upon individual and environmental conditions. On cold days, for instance, one will advance more slowly than on warm days. Morning workouts also require a longer warming-up period. Older people must progress more slowly from slow motions to more vigorous ones. One's sex is also a significant factor. Because men are generally less flexible than women, they require a greater emphasis on stretching activities to prevent muscle soreness and injuries. Due to the many modifying factors it is impossible to prescribe a specific time period for each exercise. As a rule of thumb, one should persist at each exercise until he feels that the active muscles are loosened up. Upon the conclusion of the entire warm-up and stretching session one should have achieved at least a light sweat.

Neck Circles

Begin this exercise by standing erect with your feet about shoulder width apart and your hands on your hips. First, a series of head flexions (Fig. 3-1A) and extensions (a) are executed. Next, move your head repeatedly from side (B) to side (b). Finally, combine the two motions to produce the neck circles (C). Each of the three exercises should be performed gently in the initial stages with a gradual increase in range of motion and forcefulness.

The advanced trainee can increase the tension of the exercises by resisting the movements of the head with his or her own hands. A training partner can also assist in offering resistance. Either helps strengthen the neck muscles.

Fig. 3-1. Neck circles

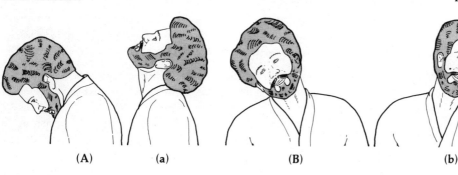

| (A) | (a) | (B) | (b) | (C) |

Fig. 3-2.
Push-ups (A) regular; (B) modified

Push-Ups

This exercise is performed a bit differently than the standard push-ups. Note that the hands are formed into fists (Fig. 3-2A). This strengthens the wrists in addition to the chest, shoulder, and arm (triceps) muscles. Since striking and blocking with the hands is a large part of karate, it is necessary that wrist strength be developed.

Many people will find the basic push-up as shown in (A) too difficult to do. Figure 3-2 (B) therefore shows a modification that is much easier to perperform. The latter is as effective in developing the involved muscles for the weaker person as the more difficult push-up is for the stronger person. One should not feel ashamed in doing them. Even for those who have no trouble in performing regular push-ups, it is desirable to begin with the easier ones for the warm-up effect. When one becomes fatigued from doing the regular push-ups, it is a good idea from the standpoint of endurance training to continue doing as many of the easier ones as possible.

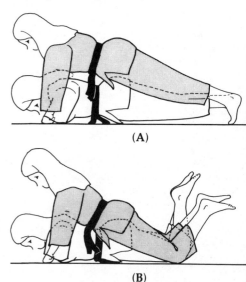

(A)

(B)

Trunk Twisting

In addition to stretching the muscles of the trunk, this exercise also stretches the muscles of the chest, shoulders, and arms. In trunk twisting (Fig. 3-3), the action of your hips should precede that of your arms. Even when the twisting actions become more vigorous, allow the involved muscles to relax as much as possible, especially at positions (B) and (D), so that the muscles will be further stretched with the ballistic whipping action.

Fig. 3-3. Trunk twisting

(A)   (B)

(C)   (D)

Wrist Circles

Wrist circles (Fig. 3-4) loosen up the wrist joints as well as develop the muscles of the forearm. By extending the arms directly in front of the body or out to the sides, the shoulder muscles can also be strengthened.

First, alternately extend (A) and flex (a) your wrist joints. After several repetitions, flex your wrists alternately in the direction of the little finger (B) and in the direction of the thumb (b). Finally, combine the two movements to result in the wrist circle action (C). For total flexibility, your wrists should be rotated in both directions. This exercise can be performed with the hands formed into fists or with open hands as shown in these illustrations.

As with the other exercises, begin each movement rather gently and progressively increase the force to produce optimal stretching and warming up. Upon completion of the exercises, relax your forearms and shake your hands vigorously.

Fig. 3-4. Wrist circles

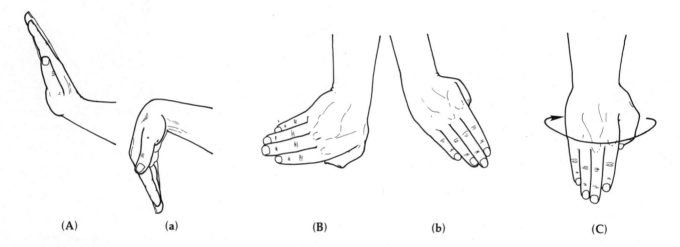

(A)   (a)   (B)   (b)   (C)

Finger Presses

Throughout this exercise your fingers are spread wide apart (Fig. 3-5). *Press* the fingers of one hand against the corresponding fingers of the opposing hand (A). Beginning with very little force, gradually increase the tension (B) until your palms are forced together (C). Even at this point, your fingers should continue to exert considerable pressure against each other. After a few seconds reduce the tension and repeat the process.

Upon completion of the exercises, relax your hands and shake them vigorously.

(A)

(B)

(C)

Fig. 3-5. Finger presses

Fig. 3-6. Sit-ups

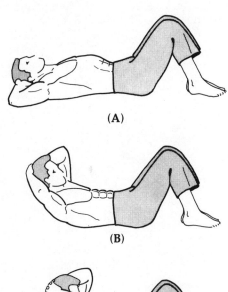

(A)

(B)

(C)

Sit-Ups

Although sit-ups are a part of most training regimens, the vast majority of athletes execute this basic exercise incorrectly. Figure 3-6 (A and C, respectively) shows the proper starting and finishing positions. Most people believe they should touch their knees with their elbows. Such practice actually reduces the tension in the abdominal muscles, because another muscle group is involved in moving the upper body from (C) to the elbow-knee position. *Tension* must be present to produce muscular improvement. For this reason one should not continue any further than (C) in performing sit-ups. Also, doing sit-ups in the elbow-knee position often causes an abrasive wound at the "tail bone" and sometimes even results in chronic muscular soreness in the lumbar (lower back) region.

Even well-trained athletes are amazed at the fitness benefits of properly executed sit-ups (Fig. 3-6). To do this, slowly move from (A) to (C) with a brief hesitation at both the starting (A) and finishing (C) positions. Exhale as you slowly curl your body up to position (C) and inhale as you return to (A). The number of sit-ups an individual should do depends upon the condition of the abdominal muscles. Beginners are advised to stop doing sit-ups before the muscles become excessively fatigued. A trained athlete, on the other hand, should continue until a strong burning sensation is experienced in the abdominal muscles and he or she is forced to stop.

Hip Twisting

In the starting position (Fig. 3-7A) place your hands at the sides of your hips for increased stability. Turn your knees first to one side (B) and then to the other (D). This twisting motion should generally be continued until the individual feels a slight burning sensation in the abdominal muscles. A serious, well-conditioned athlete will persist until the burning sensation becomes so discomforting that he is forced to stop. This combination of leg raises and trunk twisting places the full effort of the exercise directly on the abdominal muscles, which are exercised from every angle in a minimum period of time.

From the standpoint of good health, it is more important for the abdominal muscles to be strong and fit than any other skeletal muscle group in the body. Although there are a number of abdominal exercises, sit-ups and hip twisting are the most effective for strengthening the entire group of abdominal muscles.

Fig. 3-7. Hip twisting

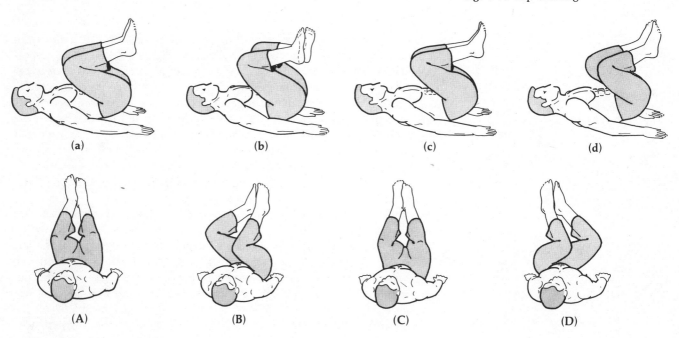

(a)   (b)   (c)   (d)

(A)   (B)   (C)   (D)

Hip Circles

Hip circles (Fig. 3-8) are employed to increase the range of motion in the hip joints by stretching the associated muscles and tendons. From the starting stance (C), begin by moving the hips in a series of side-to-side movements (A and a). The force of the movements should increasingly intensify. Next, without moving the feet, move the hips in a forward and back motion (B and b) with the greatest emphasis on the back bends. Then combine the two

Fig. 3-8. Hip circles

motions to produce the hip circle action (C). As with all exercises you should begin with slow movements. Then, as you feel the joints loosening up, continue the exercise with increasing vigor and range of motion.

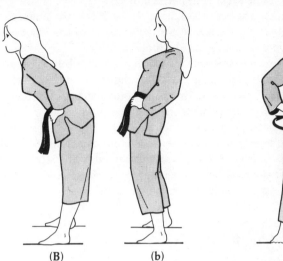

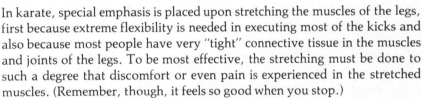

(A)   (a)   (B)   (b)   (C)

(A)

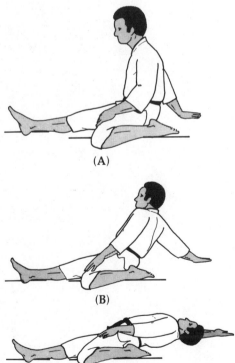

(B)

(C)

Thigh Stretches

In karate, special emphasis is placed upon stretching the muscles of the legs, first because extreme flexibility is needed in executing most of the kicks and also because most people have very "tight" connective tissue in the muscles and joints of the legs. To be most effective, the stretching must be done to such a degree that discomfort or even pain is experienced in the stretched muscles. (Remember, though, it feels so good when you stop.)

Do not attempt to achieve a high level of flexibility overnight. This component of physical fitness is improved little by little over a period of many months. In trying to hasten the process one commonly over-stretches a muscle and injures it. A setback of at least several weeks is the usual result.

The thigh-stretch exercise (Fig. 3-9) is excellent for stretching the quadriceps muscles on the front part of the thighs. Assume the starting position (A) and lean to the rear as far as the resulting discomfort or pain will permit. For the beginner this will usually be at approximately the position indicated in (B). Observe that his left hand is on the floor to provide the necessary support while he concentrates on relaxing the left quadriceps muscle. Karatekas should strive to ultimately achieve position (C). After stretching the muscles of the left thigh, reverse the positions of the legs and stretch the right quadriceps muscle.

Fig. 3-9. Thigh stretches

Chinese Splits

Chinese splits (Fig. 3-10) stretch the muscles of the inner thigh and are absolutely necessary if one expects to perform high kicks to the side (see Figs. 5-32 and 5-33) which are essential karate skills. While the average male will usually not be able to spread his legs any further than the position shown in Fig. 3-10(A), females are generally more flexible.

After your feet are eased as far apart as your flexibility will allow, bend forward at the waist, place your hands on the floor, and ease your feet still farther apart (B). Then, gradually move your hands closer to your body, and ease one hand as far under your body as possible (C). This will help maintain your balance as you proceed to slowly shift your body weight to the rear. With diligent training, one can eventually achieve the flexibility indicated in (D). A *slow* progression is demanded of the student in order to prevent injury to the muscles of the inner thigh. After completing the exercise, relax the legs and shake them vigorously.

Hamstring and Spine Stretches

Following the Chinese splits, sit on the floor with your legs spread as far apart as possible (Fig. 3-11A). By forcing the toes back towards the body, the calf muscles are stretched. From the starting position (A), slowly bend forward. When you reach the limits of your flexibility, maintain that position for a minimum of thirty seconds. Only the advanced athlete should expect to achieve position (B).

After returning to the starting position, stretch toward your right foot (C) and then toward your left foot. Hold each position for thirty seconds or longer. Ultimately, the karate student should be able to touch the forehead to each knee as shown in (C). Such extremes in flexibility generally require many months and one must progress slowly to avoid tearing the tissues being stretched. Jerky movements are definitely not recommended. If one feels personally compelled to employ bouncing motions while in positions (B) and (C), these motions should succeed the static method and be done slowly and gently.

For variety in stretching the hamstring, spine, and calf muscles, refer to the starting position for thigh stretches (Fig. 3-9). From starting position

(A)

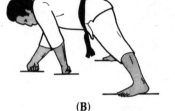

(B)

(C)

(D)

Fig. 3-10. Chinese splits

Fig. 3-11.
Hamstring and spine stretches (sitting)

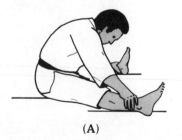

(A)

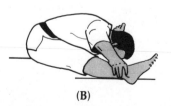

(B)

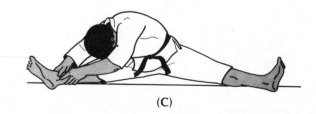

(C)

(A), instead of leaning to the rear, lean forward toward the extended foot as shown in (B) and (C) of Fig. 3-11.

Some people prefer to stretch their hamstring and spine muscles by performing the more traditional toe touching movements shown in Fig. 3-12. The difference between this sequence and the one illustrated in Fig. 3-11 is that the athlete is standing instead of sitting. Therefore, the force of gravity is of assistance in the stretching actions.

Fig. 3-12.
Hamstring and spine stretches (standing)

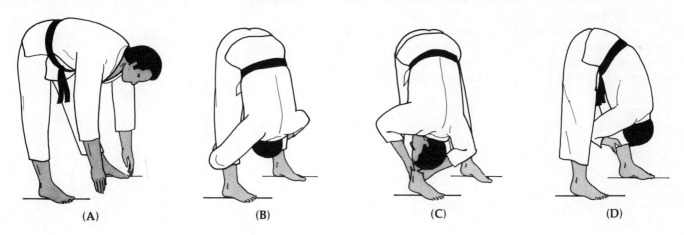

(A) (B) (C) (D)

Side Squat Stretches

This exercise stretches practically the same muscles as do the Chinese splits (Fig. 3-10). In addition, it is beneficial in making the ankle joints and leg muscles (quadriceps) more limber, which is necessary for proper foot position during the delivery of most kicks (refer to Figs. 5-32 and 5-33). In the starting position (Fig. 3-13A) the soles of the feet are flat on the floor. Shifting your weight to your right foot, lower your body. At the same time, point your left toes upward and flex (dorsiflex) the ankle so that the toes are brought toward your body (B). This action helps to stretch the hamstring and calf muscles. In the lower position (B and C) the knee of the bent leg should point directly over the toes to prevent weakening the arches of the feet. Return to the starting position several times and repeat the movement before executing a series to the opposite side.

Fig. 3-13. Side squat stretches

(A)

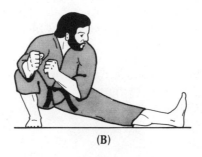

(B)

(C)

Ankle Circles

Ankle circles can be done from either a standing or a sitting position. From the starting position (Fig. 3-14A), one foot is repeatedly flexed (B) and extended (C). As usual, the initial stretching movements are rather gentle but subsequent ones are rapidly intensified. After a series of these motions, each foot, from position (D), is alternately inverted (E) and everted (F). Finally, the actions are combined to produce the ankle circle motions. Rotate each foot in both directions.

As you advance, you may prefer to perform the exercise while sitting on the floor with your feet drawn close to your body and your knees jutting out to the sides. In this position you can use both hands to force the range of motion of the ankles to slightly further extremes.

Fig. 3-14. Ankle circles

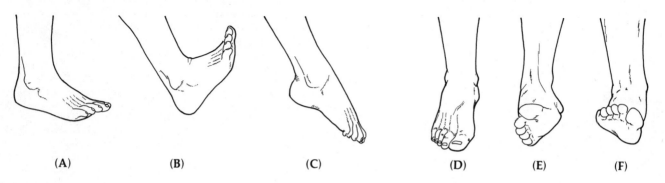

(A) (B) (C) (D) (E) (F)

Rope Jumping

Because of the endurance and muscular coordination benefits, rope jumping should be a part of every athlete's training program. Although there are hundreds of ways to jump rope, the sequence shown in Fig. 3-15 is the basic method for the "pepper rhythm."

To start the rope moving smoothly, begin with your arms forward (A). From this point, swing your arms downward and to the rear, and then continue the circular movement upward (B). As a result, your hands move in large circles with the chief points of rotation at the shoulder joints.

After the rope is moving rapidly (A through D) your arms should actually move very little. Most of the turning force for subsequent rope swings should be developed by wrist action. Note that the hands remain close to the hips (D and E). Some movement of the forearms is allowed but the main action is in the wrists.

From (F) the rope continues to (D) and the cycle is repeated for as long as you desire. You should land on the balls of your feet and spring upward in a rebounding action. To achieve the correct rhythm most of the action must occur at the ankle joints, not at the knee joints.

Fig. 3-15.
Basic rope jumping (pepper rhythm)

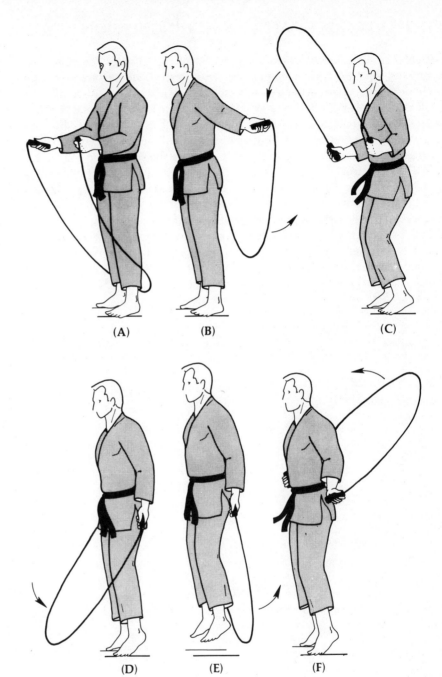

(A)   (B)   (C)

(D)   (E)   (F)

TYPICAL WARM-UP AND STRETCHING SESSION

For each of the fourteen exercises described in this chapter the suggested number of repetitions and the approximate time requirements are presented in the following chart. After you have trained enough to be aware of your individual warm-up requirements, you should adjust the program to more suitably meet your *own* needs. Some students will find that they have to concentrate more on leg stretching while others will need to devote proportionately more time to doing push-ups to increase the strength in their chest and arm muscles.

There should be very little rest between exercises as one progresses through the warm-up. Note in the list below that a *total* of only two minutes is alloted for resting. As a result, if sufficient effort is exerted one should be sweating to at least a moderate extent. Remember, the warm-up and stretching session outlined here is the *minimum* suggested routine.

Considerable space has been devoted to warming-up and stretching. This is clear evidence of the importance that must be given to these activities. They *must* precede every karate training session.

Exercise	Repetitions	Time
1. Neck Circles		
forward and back	8 cycles	30 sec.
side-to-side	8 cycles	
circles	8 in each direction	
2. Push-ups		
modified	5–10	1 min.
regular	as many as possible (to 30)	
modified	as many as possible	
3. Trunk Twisting	25 cycles	30 sec.
4. Wrist Circles		
flexion and extension	10 cycles	30 sec.
side-to-side	10 cycles	
circles	10 in each direction	
5. Finger Presses	5 (3 sec. each)	15 sec.
6. Sit-ups	as many as possible (to 50)	2 min.
7. Hip Twisting	as many as possible (to 50)	1 min.
8. Hip Circles		
side-to-side	15	1 min.
back bends	10	
circles	10 in each direction	
9. Thigh Stretches	one for each leg	1 min.

	Exercise	Repetitions	Time
10.	Chinese Splits	one without using hands one with hands on floor	1 min. 1½ min.
11.	Hamstring and Spine Stretches front side	 one one for each side	 30 sec. 30 sec./side
12.	Side Squat Stretches	3 to each side	30 sec. (total)
13.	Ankle Circles flexion and extension side-to-side circles	 10 cycles 10 cycles 10 in each direction	 30 sec.
14.	Rope Jumping	200 jumps	2½ min.
	Total Time For Exercises		approximately 15 min.
	Total Time, including periods between exercises		approximately 17 min.

4 BASIC PRINCIPLES OF KARATE MOVEMENT

Though one may possess great muscular strength and endurance, these components must be effectively utilized to produce a skillful athlete. Since efficient movement must be in harmony with the laws of physics that deal with equilibrium, motion, and force, it is highly desirable that the karate player have at least a basic understanding of these laws. Besides knowing *how* to execute the various karate punches, kicks, and blocks, the student needs to understand *why* they must be performed in specific and precise ways. In this chapter therefore a general view of the principles of body mechanics will be presented and explained. Physiological principles (those having to do with the way the human body functions) closely related to movement will also be discussed at appropriate times. For clarification, an application to karate will accompany most principles.

EQUILIBRIUM (BALANCE)

Stances are the most fundamental aspects of karate training. Further, since balance is the key to a proper stance, it is logical to begin this chapter on he-chanics with a discussion of the principles that relate to equilibrium.

In discussing eqilibrium or balance, an understanding of the concept of *center of gravity* is fundamental. Defined as the point at which the apity is the point from which the body can be held in perfect balance. In an average man standing at rest, the approximate location of the center of gravity is in the center of the body at about the level of the navel. In women, the center of gravity is generally a bit lower (Fig. 4-1A). Of course, the exact location varies according to individual body build. A person with heavy legs, for instance, will have a lower center of gravity than one with thinner legs. Furthermore, an individual can change the center of gravity location merely by changing the position of one or more parts of the body, as indicated in (B) and (C). It can even be shifted *outside* the body (D).

Fig. 4-1.
Although the location of one's *center of gravity* can easily be shifted, in all cases body weight is evenly divided above and below the point, and also is equally distributed to the left and right side of the point.

(A) (B) (C) (D)

STABILITY

Stability, one's degree of equilibrium, is closely related to the center of gravity. Since an individual can control his or her center-of-gravity location, it follows that stability can also be controlled. Sometimes it is necessary to increase positional stability, while at other times stability must be reduced or eliminated. For example, to deliver a blow with great force, one should be in a very stable stance, while to move the body rapidly one should be in an unstable position. Obviously, a knowledge and application of the principles that follow will be of great value to the karate player.

The center of gravity of an object must fall within the boundaries of its base of support for equilibrium to exist (Fig. 4-2). However, all parts of the base do not necessarily have to be in contact with the ground. When one is standing, for instance, with both feet on the ground, the base includes the area between them as well as the area of direct contact.

Stability is inversely proportional to the distance of the body's center of gravity above the base. That is, the closer one's center of gravity is to the base of support, the greater the stability. In Fig. 4-3, (B) is thus more stable than (A).

Stability is directly proportional to the area of the base upon which a body rests. Therefore, as one increases the area of the base of support, stability increases. This explains why an individual is more stable when standing flatfooted (Fig. 4-4A) than when standing merely on the front part of his feet (B). In comparing the stances seen in (C) and (D), the only difference is the turned-out position of the right foot in (D) which enlarges the area of the base. One is thus in a more stable position than he would be in stance (C). Additional control of one's balance can be gained merely by pushing with the toes (D).

Fig. 4-2.
For equilibrium, one's center of gravity must fall within one's base of support. (Base of support is indicated by dashed lines.)

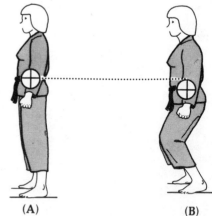

(A)   (B)

Fig. 4-3.
The lower one's center of gravity is relative to the base of support, the greater one's stability.

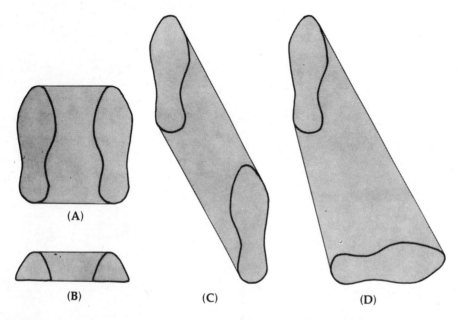

(A)

(B)   (C)   (D)

Fig. 4-4.
Stability is directly proportional to the area of one's base of support

Fig. 4-5.
Heavier people are more stable.

Fig. 4-6.
Stability in a given direction is directly proportional to the horizontal distance of the center of gravity from that edge of the base. Figure (B) is less stable than (A) in the forward direction, but more stable in the rearward direction. ▶

Stability is directly proportional to one's body weight. That is, with all other factors being equal, a heavier person (Fig. 4-5A) is more stable than a lighter one (B). Consequently, a heavier person is harder to push off balance, and is better able to punch from a more solid position. On the other hand, a lighter person, due to his relative instability, has the advantage of being able to move his or her body more rapidly in any direction (assuming, again, that all other factors are equal).

Stability in a given direction is directly proportional to the horizontal distance of the center of gravity from that edge of the base. Thus, a person who keeps his or her center of gravity over the exact center of the base (Fig. 4-6A and a) has equal stability in all directions. However, if an individual stands so that the center of gravity falls nearer the toes, stability increases in the rearward direction but decreases in the forward direction (B and b). In the latter position (B) one is able to punch more forcefully while also being in an excellent position for forward movement.

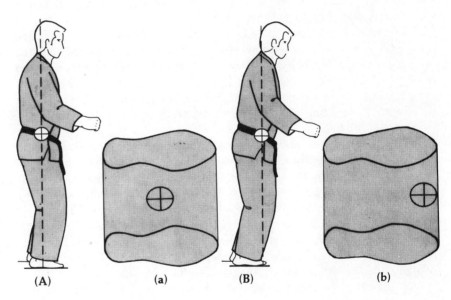

MOTION

Motion is sometimes thought of as being the opposite of equilibrium since for movement to occur equilibrium must be destroyed. The chief components of motion are speed and accuracy.

Speed

Karatekas continually strive to improve the speed of their movements so their punches and kicks will be able to score and their blocks will be in position fast enough to protect them from being scored upon.

It is a physical law that *a body at rest will remain at rest unless acted upon by a force.* In the human body, this force is produced by the contraction of muscles. Furthermore, *the speed of motion is directly proportional to the force that produced the motion.* That is, the more forcefully the muscles contract, the faster the resulting movement will be. With this in mind, it is quite obvious the karate player who desires to increase his or her speed must work to develop muscular strength.

Muscles become stronger only when they contract more forcefully than the levels to which they are commonly accustomed. The stimulus that results in muscular growth is the degree of tension in the fibers of the muscles. One way to increase the level of tension is to increase the resistance against which muscles act. Weight training is the most popular resistive exercise method. Unknown to most people, but substantiated by research, weight training when *properly* pursued improves the trainee's reaction time, flexibility, and speed as well as strength.

Muscular strength can be improved by using less resistance but contracting the muscles more rapidly. Again, the increased tension produced in the muscles stimulates a gain in strength.

So, one can view strength and speed as being different sides of the same coin; practicing one improves the other. It is therefore suggested that the serious karate student include resistive exercises in his training program and during karate practice, execute punches, kicks, and blocks with high muscular tension. The student can accomplish the latter by moving very fast or by moving slowly, but with strongly contracted muscles, a technique commonly referred to as *dynamic tension.*

To most effectively utilize the speed that is produced by muscular contraction, one must closely adhere to sound principles of mechanics. To execute any movement in the shortest possible time, the most important rule is for the movement to occur along a straight line to its final destination. This very simple but significant principle is based upon the fact that *the shortest distance between two points is a straight line.* Consider the technique of the karate athlete who wants to strike a target with his fist (Fig. 4-7). From the ready position (A) to the point of contact (B) the fist should travel along a straight line for the fastest strike.

If, of course, the target is out of the range of one's fist, it is necessary to step toward it. For the reasons mentioned above, one's feet must also move in a direct and straight line to cover the distance as rapidly as possible.

If one steps directly toward the target, it would seem that the body (or more specifically the body's center of gravity) would also move in a straight path. This would certainly be desirable, but unless a person is quite skillful such motion will not occur. True, the center of gravity apparently travels in a straight line when viewed from overhead; however, when viewed from the front or side, this direct motion rarely occurs. In Fig. 4-8 (A)–(E), observe the path of the center of gravity in an average person taking a step forward. Obviously, the center of gravity is moving up and down as well as forward. Due to the extraneous movement, time is wasted. In everyday sit-

Fig. 4-7.
For the fastest punch, a fist should travel along a straight line from the ready position to the target.

uations the split-second increase in movement time is of little importance. For the karate participant, however, it is vital to success. Mere fractions of a second make the difference, offensively, between scoring and not scoring and, defensively, between being struck and not being struck.

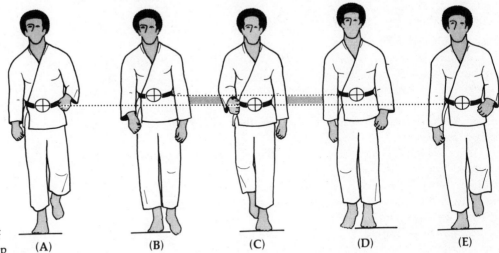

Fig. 4-8.
Movement of the body's center of gravity in a typical forward step

(A)   **(B)**   **(C)**   **(D)**   **(E)**

Figure 4-9 shows how the karateka is able to increase the speed of forward movement by stepping so that his center of gravity moves in a more direct line even when viewed from the front or side. Body movements to the rear and sides should, when possible, conform to the same principle. Such movements may seem rather unorthodox or even humorous to the uninformed, but they are based upon sound body mechanics and are most effective. Note in Fig. 4-9 that the angle of the left foot in (A) is identical to its angle in (B) and (C). By maintaining this position, extraneous movement, including the up and down motion of the center of gravity, is eliminated.

Fig. 4-9.
Movement of the body's center of gravity in a forward karate step

(A)   **(B)**   **(C)**   **(D)**   **(E)**   **(F)**

Accuracy

Not only must karatekas be able to move rapidly to be successful, they must move with *accuracy*. To accomplish this, they must *keep their eyes open and their opponents in view*. By observing an opponent's offensive movement from its earliest point, defensive action can be initiated at the earliest possible moment by either blocking or retreating. For purposes of deception, it is not always wise to look directly at the target, but it should at least be viewed through one's peripheral vision.

Accuracy, as well as speed, is reduced when muscles are fatigued. Too strenuous a warm-up is detrimental to high-level performances. Unfortunately, some trainees are so physically unfit that even a mild warm-up is exhausting, and they are not able to devote much effort to learning the karate skills. As their physical condition improves, they will be able to practice for longer periods.

Even the most finely conditioned athletes, though, eventually become fatigued. Along with the beginners, they should be aware of the dangers of fatigue, namely, reduced muscular coordination and accuracy. One's punches and kicks must be delivered with precise control especially during sparring sessions. During these mock fighting sessions, only slight brushing contact can be permitted. In a fatigued state the probability of forceful contact is magnified, and serious injury is more likely to result. In light of this, it is strongly recommended that sparring cease upon the first signs of muscular fatigue.

FORCE

Force is the effort one body exerts against another and it is intimately related to motion. In fact, motion is created only through the application of force. Conversely, motion ceases or is reduced solely by retarding forces.

In the human body force is developed through muscular contractions. The stronger a muscle is, the more forcefully it can contract. Since forceful actions, both offensively and defensively, are required in karate, it is again strongly recommended thet one work to increase the strength of his muscles. As previously stated in the section on motion (page 46), such increases can be achieved through a resistive exercise program, as well as by executing the karate movements with speed and vigor.

Available Force and Speed

Stated concisely, *available force varies inversely with speed of movement*. In other words, the faster a muscle shortens during contraction, the less force available for overcoming a resistance. This is based on the fact that there is a limited amount of tension that can be developed within a muscle. If a large portion of that tension is used for rapid shortening, only a rela-

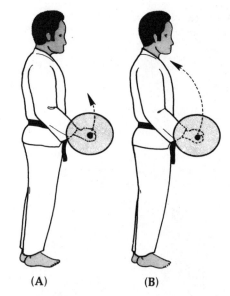

(A)   **(B)**

Fig. 4-10.
Available force varies inversely with the speed of movement. (A) Here the muscle's energy is being used primarily to overcome the resistance offered by the *heavy* weight. Little energy remains for rapid shortening of the muscle. (B) Here the weight is very *light*. Therefore, much of the muscle's energy is available for rapid shortening.

tively small amount of the tension can be utilized to develop the force necessary to overcome a heavy resistance. Conversely, if the tension is used primarily to exert a force, little will be available for producing fast movements. If the validity of this concept is doubted, one merely has to experiment with lifting both light and heavy dumbbells as show in Fig. 4-10.

In karate, while a blow is being delivered (Fig. 4-11A, B, and C), most of the energy of the involved muscles should be used for shortening. Maximum speed of delivery is thus attained.

As the foot nears the target (D), much of the energy should immediately be used to develop great force upon contact with the target. Also, the greater the resistance offered to the blow the more forceful the blow should be. Strikes to the head, for instance, require less energy transference from speed to force than do those to the body.

Converting energy utilization from speed to force is accomplished by powerfully and rapidly tensing the entire body just as contact is made and by continuing to exert a powerful muscular effort for the split second *after* contact with the target is made. Too often one "lets up" upon contact or just before it is made. Other principles for delivering powerful blows will be discussed in the sections that immediately follow.

Fig. 4-11.
Energy should be used primarily for speed during the delivery of a kick (or punch). Upon contact it should be used chiefly to exert a force against the target.

(A)   (B)   (C)   (D)

Summation of Forces

Many muscle groups are involved in delivering a punch or kick. If all the involved muscle groups were to contract at precisely the same instand, however, the final force would be severely limited by the weakest group. Therefore, each of the forces developed by the various muscle groups must follow a sequence that results in their being *added* together to produce the *maximal* final force.

Generally, the proper sequence is for the strongest muscle group to contract first, then the next strongest, with the weakest group contracting finally to contribute its small force. Further, each contraction must occur at an exactly prescribed moment for the maximum summation of forces to be achieved. As a rule of thumb, *each succeeding force should be started at the point of greatest velocity resulting from the preceding force.* At full speed the total movement pattern takes place so rapidly that one does not have time to think about the individual motions that make up each sequence. One may wish to occasionally practice karate skills in slow motion, though, and work on the proper sequences. In any case, one concentrates on achieving a feeling of smoothness. Some people refer to this smoothness as proper timing or rhythm. The terms are practically synonymous.

The *reverse punch* (Fig. 4-12) is used to demonstrate the proper summation of forces as they are applied in karate. The karateka in the illustration spins on the ball of his right foot while his right ankle and leg extend (A) allowing his right hip to rotate forward (B). In (B), as the hip achieves its greatest velocity, the right shoulder begins its forward motion. The hip still continues to move forward a bit. Similarly, in (C) the right shoulder has already reached its greatest speed but is still moving forward as the right arm is extending toward the target. The wrist rotation that provides the final force completes its action at the point of contact (D). The trainee should work on developing the proper sequence of events in a smooth, unhesitating motion.

Fig. 4-12.
Summation of forces as they apply to the *reverse punch*

(A)	(B)	(C)	(D)

Force and Distance of Application

The longer a force is applied against an object, the greater its final velocity and the greater the force it exerts against another objeit upon contact. For example, the longer one holds one's foot on the accelerator, the faster the automobile will travel and the more forceful its impact will be against some

(A)

(B)

(C)

Fig. 4-13.
Force is directly proportional to the distance over which it is applied. (A) will therefore develop greater force upon contact than (B) or (C). (B) will make contact sooner than (A) while (C) will make fastest contact.

object such as a tree or pedestrian. This is also true in the martial arts. In Fig. 4-13(A) the figure is "rearing back" in preparatio for delivering a blow with his fist. There is no doubt, all other factors being equal, that his fist will be traveling faster and will make a more forceful contact with the target than would that of the person who initiates his punch from the position shown in (B) or (C). On the other hand, it is also obvious that the elapsed time of the movement in (A) will be of longer duration than the time in either (B) or (C). Figure (C), conversely, will strike his target before either (A) or (B) has a chance to land his punch.

Sometimes force is more important than the time factor. On other occasions, in karate competition for example, where only light contact is permitted, speed is the prime consideration. Indeed, due to the speed advantage many competitors prefer to throw the fist from a position high on the side as depicted in (C). In actual combat the movement shown in (B) is probably most effective. While it is a bit slower than (C), considerably more force can be developed at the point of contact.

Force and Direction

In order to achieve the maximum total force, each of the individual forces involved must be applied in the same direction. This principle seems logical enough, yet it is violated by many athletes in all sports.

A simple example, with just two forces being considered, should suffice in clarifying this rule. In Fig. 4-14, the first force is produced by the forward step (B), and a second step results from the arm extension (C). In Fig. 4-15,

(A)

(B)

(C)

Fig. 4-14.
Forward step and lunge punch

arrows are drawn to show the direction and magnitude of each force. The lengths of the arrows symbolizing the forward step and the straight punch (in both A and B) are all of equal length because they represent equal magnitudes of force in a given example. Note that in (A), the arrow representing the *total force* is longer than the one in (B). In (B) part of the individual forces are wasted in unproductive directions while in (A) the full effect of each of the individual forces is felt at the target.

Of course, one may purposely employ the movement depicted in (B) for reasons of deception, but the student should know that the force of his blow will be diminished.

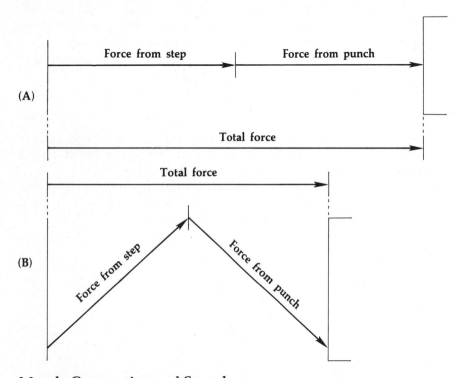

Fig. 4-15.
To achieve the maximal final force each of the individual forces must be applied in the same direction.

Muscle Contraction and Stretch

If a muscle is stretched, it will contract more forcefully than if it had not been stretched. This physiological condition occurs *only* if the stretching action *immediately* precedes the muscle contraction.

Fortunately, when the individual muscle groups come into play in their proper sequence and with precise timing (Fig. 4-12), each respective muscle group is automatically stretched just before it is to shorten. Considering just two parts of the body, for simplicity, Fig. 4-16 shows how forward rotation of the right hip (B) causes the muscles on the right side of the chest (the pectoral muscles) to be stretched. These muscles then contract more strongly than usual to bring the punching arm forward more powerfully.

Fig. 4-16.
As the right hip rapidly rotates forward, the right chest muscles are stretched. As a result, the latter then contract more forcefully than they would have without the stretch.

(A) (B) (C)

Action-Reaction

A law of physics states, "for every action there is an equal and simultaneous reaction in exactly the opposite direction." This is easily demonstrated. One merely has to stand close to a wall and place both hands against it as shown in Fig. 4-17 (A). Then, by pushing against the wall gently, your body will be forced in a rearward direction (B). This proves that while you are applying a force in the direction of the wall (arrow E), the wall is simultaneously exerting a force against you (arrow W). Further, the more forcefully you push against the wall, the more forcefully you will be pushed backwards (C), indicating that the reaction is always equal to the action.

Obviously, you cannot push too forcefully against the wall from the stance shown in (A, B, and C) or you will fall off balance to the rear. A person can, however, greatly increase his or her ability to exert a force against the wall by simply extending one leg rearward to act as a brace (D).

Fig. 4-17.
When one exerts a force against a wall it exerts an equal force against him.

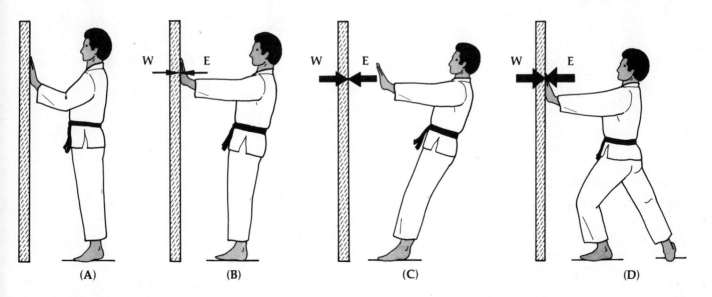

(A) (B) (C) (D)

True, as one increases the force of one's push, the wall will also increase its opposite force. One will not fall backwards, though, because the harder the back foot pushes against the floor, the harder the floor pushes back.

To apply the action-reaction principle to the act of punching, refer to Fig. 4-18. From the stance in (A), relatively little force can be exerted because the puncher will be forced to the rear (B) as her fist strikes the target. From the stance shown in (C) the athlete can deliver a more forceful blow. If she allows the bracing leg to bend at the moment of contact (D), however, the force will be diminished because the bending action will permit her to be pushed backwards. By keeping the bracing leg perfectly straight and rigid upon contact (D) she prevents herself from being shoved rearward and thus can deliver a punch with greater force. Not only should the leg be rigid but the entire body should be rigid at the moment of contact with the target. This principle, based on the law of action-reaction, should be strictly adhered to whenever one wishes to land a blow with considerable force.

Another point is demonstrated by the girl's stance in (C). By keeping her abdomen (or navel) thrust forward, the girl keeps her center of gravity nearer the leading edge of her front foot (refer to Fig. 4-6). This creates greater stability in a rearward direction, which in turn improves her action-reaction capability. At the same time, since she is less stable in the forward direction, she is able to move forward more rapidly.

Fig. 4-18.
To prevent the body from being pushed backwards by the reactive force of a blow, the rear leg should be forcefully straightened at the moment of contact. Indeed, the entire body should be momentarily rigid at contact.

(A)　　　　　(B)　　　　　(C)　　　　　(D)

Force-Pressure Relationship

Although two persons may strike a target with equal force, one may make contact with a pressure that is many times greater than the other and therefore deliver a more effective blow. One increases the pressure of a blow by concentrating his or her force to a smaller area of contact. The formula below shows that pressure, upon contact, depends upon the magnitude of

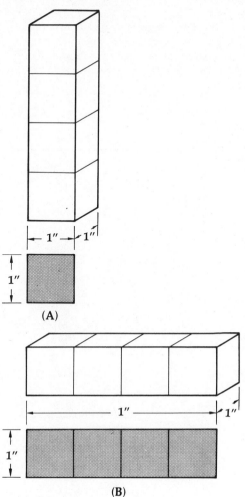

(A)

(B)

the force as well as on the area over which the force is distributed. Stated more specifically, pressure can be increased by increasing the force or by reducing the area of contact.

$$\text{Pressure} = \frac{\text{Force}}{\text{Area}}$$

Figure 4-19 is used to clarify the force-pressure relationship. Each of the blocks represents a one-inch cube weighing one pound. In (A), four blocks are stacked vertically so a force of four pounds is exerted over the base area of one square inch. The pressure on the base of support, therefore, equals four pounds per square inch. In (B), the four cubes are arranged horizontally so that the force of four pounds is spread over a base of four square inches. The resulting pressure in this case equals one pound per square inch. So, even though the forces against the bases of support in both (A) and (B) are equal, the pressure exerted in (A) is four times greater than in (B).

Since karate is a *martial* art, one must learn ways to deal as much damage as possible to an opponent. Increasing the force of one's blows is one way to accomplish this end and many principles have previously been discussed to help in this endeavor. Since there is a limit to the amount of force an individual can generate, this section is devoted to showing how to increase the *effect* of this force by merely decreasing the area of contact. For instance, in board-breaking demonstrations a karate expert strikes the board *not* with the open palm (Fig. 4-20B), but with the relatively thin side of the hand (A).

Fig. 4-19.
The pressure exerted at a point of contact depends upon the force and the area of contact.

Fig. 4-20.
In board-breaking demonstrations the force of the hand (or foot) should be concentrated in a small area as depicted in (A).

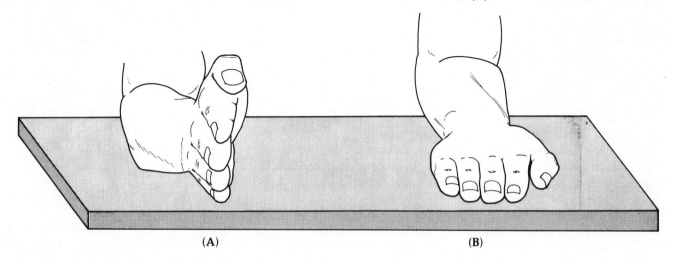

(A)   (B)

The force-pressure concept explains the devastating effect of a karate punch. Normally, when one punches an opponent the area of contact will be the entire width of a fist as indicated in Fig. 4-21(A) and the shaded area of (a). In karate, however, the front of the fist is canted downward a bit (B) so the area of contact is limited to the area of the two protruding knuckles (shaded areas of b). Similarly, the effect of a kick that makes contact as demonstrated in Fig. 4-22 (B and b) will be greater than the one shown in (A and a).

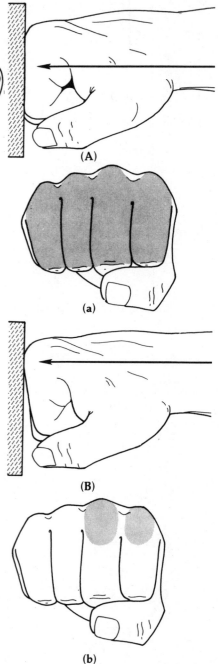

Fig. 4-21.
Greater pressure is exerted upon contact when the area of contact of a punch is reduced. The shaded areas indicate the areas of contact. Compare (a) with (b).

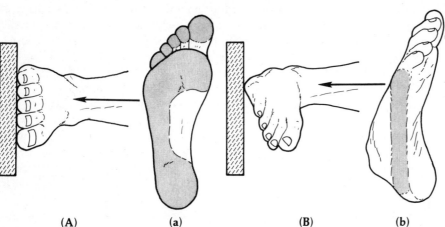

(A)   (a)   (B)   (b)

Fig. 4-22.
Greater pressure is exerted upon contact when the area of contact of a kick is reduced. The shaded areas indicate the areas of contact. Compare (a) with (b).

Dissipation of Force

While athletes are often required to develop skills that can produce high levels of force, there are many situations that call for forces, upon contact, to be reduced. First, force can be dissipated by absorbing it over a distance; in other words, one can "give" with a force. Catching a ball is an excellent example. When the man in Fig. 4-23 reaches out with his hands to make contact with the ball (A), he absorbs its force by slowing down its velocity as he brings his hands toward his chest (B and C).

The *effect* of a force can also be reduced by distributing it over a larger area, thus reducing the pressure that occurs at contact. This procedure is best exemplified in the sport of judo. If a person is thrown to the floor, and lands as in Fig. 4-24(A), the force of the landing would almost certainly result in serious injury. A judo devotee, therefore, spends many hours learning to land so that the force of his falls will be spread over a large area of his body. A typical judo position for landing is shown in (B).

Fig. 4-23.
Force can be absorbed over a distance to reduce its effect.

(A)

(B)

(C)

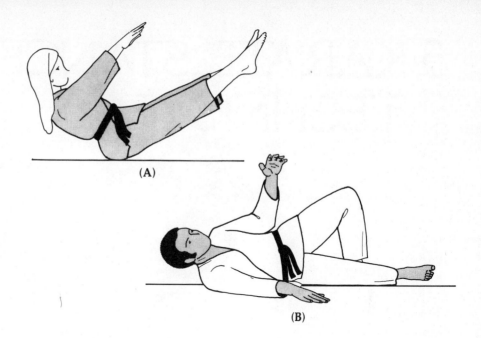

(A)

(B)

Fig. 4-24.
The effect of a force (upon landing, for instance) can be reduced by increasing the area of contact. Compare (A) with (B).

In karate, self-defense can be achieved by avoiding or blocking the opponent's blows or by leaning or stepping backwards so the force of a blow, when it does make contact, is absorbed over a greater distance. Unfortunately, beginners frequently violate this principle by injudiciously charging forward just as the opponent is delivering a punch or kick. Stepping into a blow will, of course, greatly magnify the force of contact.

SUMMARY

All efficient physical skill is based upon proper utilization of the physical laws of mechanics. It therefore behooves the serious karateka to acquire at least a fundamental knowledge and understanding of physical laws, especially as they apply to his sport. It may well mean the difference between success and failure.

Although a complete presentation of the principles of mechanics dealing with equilibrium, motion, and force is not within the scope of this book, the pertinent ones have been discussed. Hopefully, upon completion of this book, one will not only know *how* the basic karate skills are performed, but will also have an understanding of *why* they are executed a particular way and why a punch or kick is not always delivered in the same way.

5 KARATE STANCES AND TECHNIQUES

Karate skills can be divided into two main categories, stances and techniques. Stances simply refer to *body positions*. Each new stance involves a change in the center of gravity and in the placement of one's feet. Techniques have to do with *actions* such as punches, strikes, kicks, and blocks. It is neither feasible, nor necessary, to present every conceivable stance and technique in this basic text, but the most common and important ones are included. A clear explanation of each skill is shown by photographs.

The names of the stances and techniques discussed in this book are the anglicized versions. They are as accurate as the Oriental terms and are more meaningful to the English-speaking person. For the purist, however, the Japanese and Korean terms appear in the Glossary.

When performing karate skills one should be aware of the muscular actions of the body and learn to *enjoy* them. Although this kinesthetic feeling originates at sensory receptors located in the muscles, joints, and tendons, it is interpreted in the brain as a delightfully euphoric experience that envelops the entire body. Call it a "high" if you wish, and if you develop a lifelong addiction to it—*fine*. Such movement is very healthy for an individual, emotionally as well as physically.

Just as painting and music training instills an appreciation of visual and auditory stimuli, karate training is an excellent opportunity for an individual to acquire an *appreciation* of movement. Some people develop an appreciation of their environments, external and internal, without special instruction. For others, such training is invaluable, since many people need just a nudge to awaken their awareness of the beauty around and within them. Just making the karateka realize the existence of the kinesthetic, or "muscle" sense, is often sufficient to initiate him or her into perceiving the joys of movement. From a purely practical standpoint, movement can become so pleasant that one ceases to see training sessions as *work* that must be endured to acquire skill, but rather as very pleasant, though demanding, experiences.

STANCES

The most fundamental karate skills are the *stances*, because all karate techniques are delivered from these precise body positions. And since no single stance is effective in all situations, several, at least, must be learned. Some stances are better for defensive purposes, while others are generally superior for offensive actions. Some allow one to move forward very quickly, while others permit more rapid movement to either the sides or the rear. All correct stances, though, require the following:

1. facing the proper direction,
2. shoulders relaxed,
3. abdomen tensed,
4. back straight and erect.

When viewing the photographs of stances in this section, keep in mind that practically any hand and arm position can be used for each stance. A variety of arm positions are shown with the stances to stress the point. Again, stances have to do primarily with the positions of the hips, legs, and feet.

Attention Stance

Sometimes called the closed or normal stance, the attention stance (Fig. 5-1) is used primarily as preparation for the ceremonial bow (refer to Fig. 2-8). The feet should be parallel to each other and touching (B). One's body weight should be equally distributed on the balls and heels of both feet. Techniques are seldom delivered from this stance.

Ready Stance

The ready, or natural, stance (Fig. 5-2) is assumed by students whenever they are receiving instructions from the teacher. It is also usually employed as the beginning and finishing stance for karate forms. Hold your fists a bit forward of the body and your feet about shoulder width apart, turned out slightly (B). Weight should be equally distributed on the balls and heels of both feet. As with the attention stance, techniques are seldom delivered from the ready stance. However, because these stances are often used, karatekas should be aware of their names and correct execution.

(A)   (a)

(B)

Fig. 5-1. Attention stance

Fig. 5-2. Ready stance

(A)   (a)

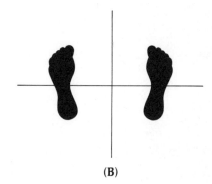

(B)

(A)

(a)

Fig. 5-3. Horse stance

Horse Stance

For obvious reasons, the horse stance (Fig. 5-3) is sometimes called the riding or straddle stance. In this particular position the knees are bent and the feet are usually about one-and-a-half to two shoulder widths apart. If your feet are any further apart than this, the stance will be weakened because rapid movement is hampered. During practice sessions, however, you may assume a wider stance (B) to help increase the flexibility of your hip joints.

Body weight should be equally distributed on the balls and heels of both feet. Force your knees outward so that a line drawn down either thigh will pass over the corresponding knee and over the toes. Unless one concentrates on doing this, the knees tend to sag inward and the result is a weak position. Incidentally, incorrect distribution will also weaken the arches of the feet.

You must tense the abdominal and gluteal (buttocks) muscles to bring the lower pelvic section forward. The latter is absolutely necessary to attain a straight and erect back posture. If the thigh muscles are weak, one will invariably lean forward at the waist to reduce the stress on the thighs. Again, this results in a poor stance. As the leg muscles become stronger, there will be less tendency to "cheat" in this manner.

Since the horse stance provides a wide base of support and a low center of gravity, it offers a very stable, well-balanced position for the lateral movements. Consequently this stance is quite effective in executing certain forceful techniques to the sides, such as the back fist, most of the blocks, side kicks, and roundhouse kicks. When an opponent is attacking a karateka from the side, the horse stance is also a sound defensive position. Only one side is exposed to the attack and fewer vital points are accessible.

(B)

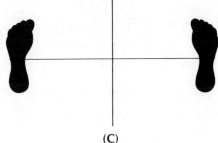

(C)

Forward Stance

The forward stance (Fig. 5-4) is frequently used. It is quite effective, both defensively and offensively, particularly for delivering techniques to the front. As with most stances, you may step forward or rearward with either foot to assume the correct position. With the right leg forward, it is called a right forward stance and, conversely, a left forward stance when the left leg is forward.

While the front leg should be bent so the shin is vertical to the floor, the rear leg must be forcefully extended so it is straight and rigid. This prevents the karateka from being pushed backward by the force of his own blow upon contact. As a result the full force of the blow is dealt to the opponent. (See action-reaction, page 53.)

To move with equal swiftness in any direction, your center of gravity should fall exactly in the center of your base of support. Each foot will thereby bear fifty percent of your weight. Sometimes you will prefer to have your center of gravity fall a bit closer to the front foot, so that it bears about sixty percent of your weight. This position permits more rapid *forward* motion and increases your stability during a forefist punch; it does, however, slow movement to the rear.

Notice in the foot pattern (B), the front foot points straight ahead while the rear foot points outward at about forty-five degrees. Typically, the rear foot is placed in a position that results in, roughly, a 110° angle between the front and rear thighs. To deliver a very powerful *low* blow, however, a karateka will usually step so that the feet are farther apart and the angle between the thighs is greater. Therefore one should devote considerable time to practicing the low forward stance to acquire the necessary flexibility.

Fig. 5-4. Forward stance

(A)　　　　　　　　　　(a)

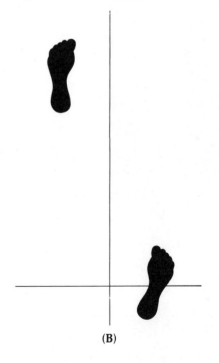

(B)

Fig. 5-5. Back stance

(A)

(a)

Laterally, the karateka's feet should be about shoulder width apart. Due to the large base of support and low center of gravity, the forward stance produces an extremely stable position for delivering powerful punches, especially in a forward direction.

Back Stance

The back stance (Fig. 5-5) is an excellent position because of its flexibility. From the back stance one can swiftly step into the other karate stances. It is also easy to assume the back stance from other stances merely by stepping forward or backward with either foot.

Many karatekas place the feet so the front foot points directly forward while the rear foot points anywhere from forty-five degrees to ninety degrees to the side (B). Others prefer to rotate the heel of the front foot about one inch out to the side. This slightly increases the area of one's base of support and thereby results in a somewhat more stable position. When the right foot is to the rear, as in Fig. 5-5, the stance is termed a right back stance. When the left foot is back, it is called a left back stance.

In the back stance, your center of gravity must be rearward and within your base of support so that about seventy percent of your weight is borne by the rear foot and thirty percent by the front one. Lower your hips and bend your rear leg about forty degrees. Force your rear knee outward a bit so that a line drawn down the thigh will pass over the knee and toes. Allowing the rear knee to sag inward is a common error which results in a weakened position. Note that the forward leg is also bent. From this position, you can propel yourself backwards merely by straightening it forcefully. Also, by bending the legs, you lower your center of gravity and the position thus becomes more stable.

To maintain a straight and erect posture in the upper body, the bottom part of the pelvis must be tucked forward. The karateka can face directly forward, as in Fig. 5-5, or he can face half-front, that is, a bit to the side.

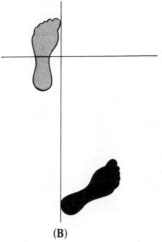

(B)

Cat Stance

Some of the early karate masters devised karate stances and techniques patterned after the movements made by wild animals. For example, a cat preparing to defend itself will often assume a position where one of its forelegs is not bearing any body weight so it is free to strike with that leg. Usually the toes will barely be touching the ground. The cat stance (Fig. 5-6) is patterned after this "ready" position.

The cat stance resembles the back stance somewhat. Note in the floor pattern (B), the front foot is brought much closer to the rear foot and only the toes of the front foot touch the floor. Nearly all of the karateka's weight is borne on the back foot, leaving the front one free to execute kicks with devastating swiftness. For this reason, the cat stance is often favored in combative situations, especially by those who have acquired considerable hip and leg flexibility through the stretching exercises discussed in Chapter Three.

To maintain the strongest position in this stance, keep your rear knee directly over your toes. Bend your rear leg just a little so your center of gravity remains high off the floor. Coupled with the small base of support, this results in a rather unstable position which, of course, is most advantageous for permitting rapid movement in any direction. Because the front leg is bent, you can propel yourself backward by straightening it forcefully. This adds to its value as a defensive stance.

When the left foot is rearward the stance is termed a left cat stance; when the right foot is back it is called a right cat stance.

  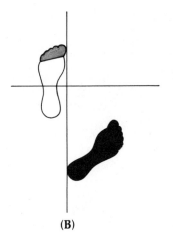

Fig. 5-6. Cat stance

(A)   (a)   (B)

Pigeon-Toe Stance

The pigeon-toe stance (Fig. 5-7) is generally used by beginners to help them develop the muscles of the legs and strengthen the knee joints. Although it is an effective stance, it is seldom used in fighting situations because a similar stance called the sanchin stance is even more effective for both forward and rearward mobility. The pigeon-toe and sanchin stances are the only ones in which the toes of both feet point inward.

Fig. 5-7. Pigeon-toe stance

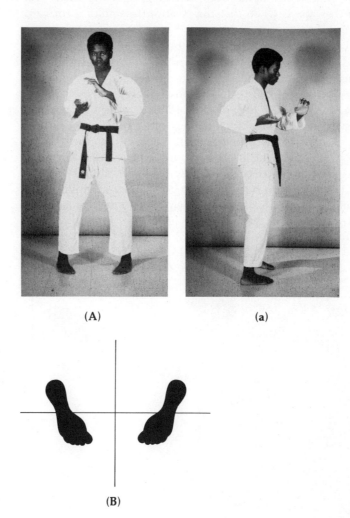

(A)

(a)

(B)

Sanchin Stance

Because the sanchin stance (Fig. 5-8) is so effective in combative situations, it is sometimes called the fighting stance. It is also known as the hour-glass stance. While there are individual preferences, the feet are usually placed about shoulder width apart with each foot pointing inward at approximately forty-five degrees. Note in foot pattern (B) that the toes of the rear foot are in line with the heel of the forward foot; however, some karatekas prefer them even further apart (C) so that the position resembles a forward stance with the toes pointing inward.

Because the knees are bent, the rest of the body is set in motion when they are extended. If the legs were straight, you would first have to bend them before extension and movement could take place. Such a maneuver is, of course, costly in terms of time. Unlike most stances, in the sanchin posture your knees are turned inward (toward each other), a position which protects the genitals from kicks. This is one of the reasons it is favored by many karatekas for actual combat. In addition, the sanchin position permits swift movement in all directions because your center of gravity falls exactly in the center of your base of support. By tucking the lower part of the pelvis forward, you will keep your center of gravity a bit higher than if you slouched. This, too, will help you to move rapidly in preparing to deliver defensive and offensive techniques. As with other stances, either foot can be rearward in the sanchin stance.

Fig. 5-8. Sanchin stance

(A)   (a)   (B)   (C)

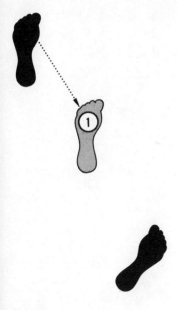

Changing Stances

After mastering the basic stances utilized in karate, the student must practice moving rapidly and smoothly from one stance to another. This ability is important for both pursuing and retreating from an opponent, and for shifting from a strong offensive posture to a more defensive one. An example of stepping from a forward stance to a back stance is seen in Fig. 5-9. Sometimes you can change stances by simply shifting your feet, for instance, from a cat stance to a sanchin stance (Fig. 5-10). On the other hand, stepping with both feet may be required as in moving to the rear from a back stance to another back stance (Fig. 5-11). Also, you can move forward from one back stance to another by reversing the procedure in Fig. 5-11. Sometimes only one foot need be moved to assume a new stance such as in shifting from a back stance to a cat stance (Fig. 5-12) where the forward foot is merely drawn back to the new placement.

In all of the foot pattern illustrations that follow, the *black* footprints indicate the initial stances while the *shaded* footprints indicate the final stances.

Fig. 5-9.
Forward stance to a back stance

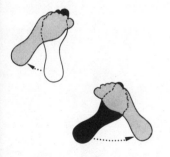

Fig. 5-10.
Cat stance to a sanchin stance

Fig. 5-12.
Back stance to a cat stance

Fig. 5-11.
Back stance to another back stance

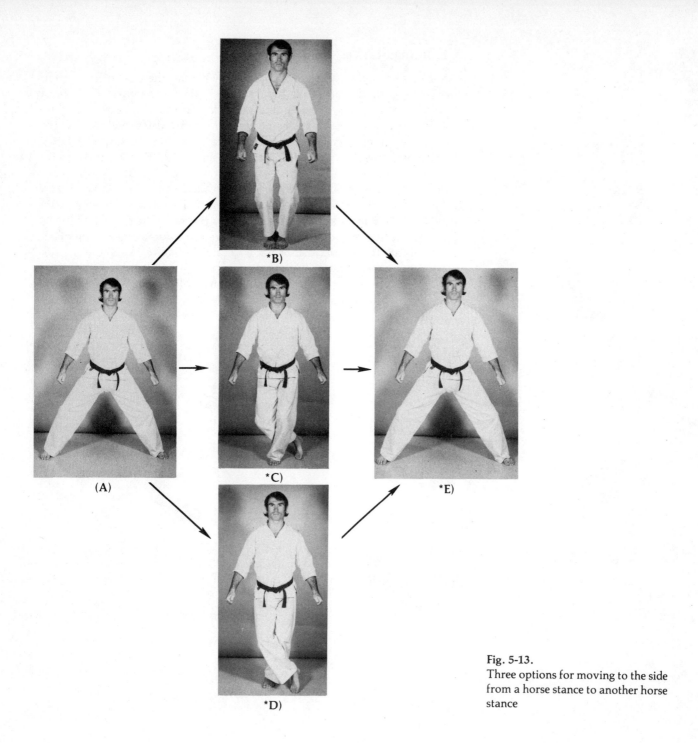

*B)

(A)

*C)

*E)

*D)

Fig. 5-13.
Three options for moving to the side from a horse stance to another horse stance

(A)

(B)

Because it is usually difficult for a beginner to move rapidly from a horse stance, Figs. 5-13 and 5-14 show how to move to the side in a horse stance and how to step efficiently into a forward stance, respectively. In moving to the side, for example to the left, the karateka has three options as shown in Fig. 5-13. He can simply bring his right foot to his left (B) and then step with his left to assume another horse stance (E). To cover a greater distance, though, he should step either behind (C) or in front (D) of his left foot before assuming another horse stance.

To step forward from a horse stance to a forward stance (Fig. 5-14) the karateka shifts his center of gravity forward and sideward toward his right foot and brings his left foot forward (B) and places it in a left forward stance (C). To assume a right forward stance the reverse procedure is, of course, followed.

One should also practice stepping from a horse stance, either forward or backward, to a back stance, cat stance, or sanchin stance.

Fig. 5-14.
Stepping from a horse stance to a left forward stance

(C)

A karateka should also be proficient at changing directions while changing stances. Figure 5-15(A) shows a foot pattern for shifting 90° to the left from one right back stance to another. First shift your center of gravity rearward and sidewards and then pivot on the right foot bringing the left foot to position #1. You can also turn in the same direction by shifting your center of gravity *forward* and sidewards, pivoting on the left foot, and stepping with the right foot forward to again assume a right back stance.

Figure 5-15 (B) shows the foot pattern for similarly shifting 90° to the right, again from one right back stance, to another. First shift your center of gravity forward and to the left, and then pivot on the ball of the left foot while bringing the right foot back to position #1. You can also turn 90° by pivoting on the right foot and bringing the left foot back to assume a *left* back stance. Using either (A) and (B) of Fig. 5-15, you can also execute a 180° turn merely by rotating further on the pivoting foot and bringing the other foot further around before placing it in position for another back stance; you can even change to a forward, cat, or sanchin stance.

Fig. 5-15.
Examples of turning from a back stance to another back stance

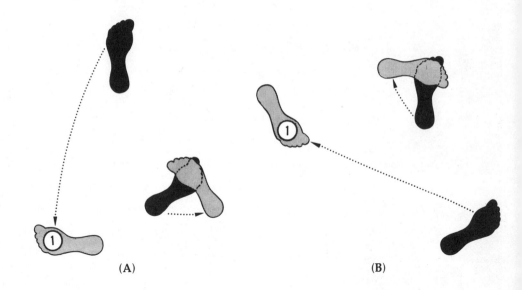

(A)   (B)

Other examples of turning are given in Fig. 5-16 using the forward stance. From the initial position in (A), shift your weight forward and to the left, pivot on the left foot, and bring the right foot back 90° to position #1 to assume another *left* forward stance. In (B) one accomplishes the 90° turn by stepping *forward* and to the side with the right foot to position #1, while pivoting on the left. Of course, these turns should be practiced from a *right* forward stance as well as from the *left* forward stance shown here.

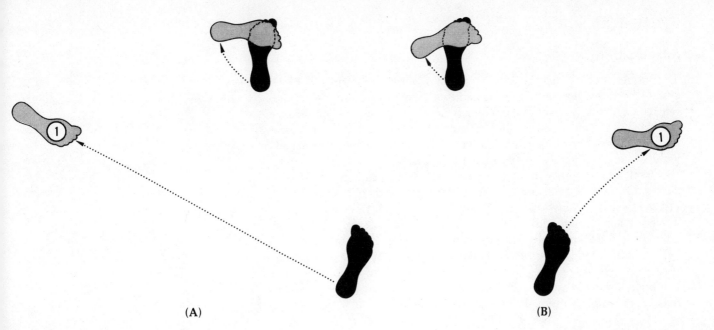

(A)   (B)

Fig. 5-16.
Examples of turning from a forward
stance to another forward stance.

All stances should be practiced moving forward, rearward, and laterally. You should also work on shifting from one type of stance to another. Many stance changes are obviously possible, and it certainly is not feasible to describe them all there. Several examples have been illustrated, though; and some general rules follow:

1. *Look* before turning.

2. In changing stances there is always a shift in the position of the feet and in the body's *center of gravity.*

3. The center of gravity must begin shifting immediately, *before* the feet move.

4. All movements must be *smooth* and *rapid.*

5. When stepping, your feet should not be lifted high off the floor nor should they drag. The action can be best described as a *gliding* movement.

6. The upper body must maintain an *erect* posture at all times when changing stances.

Stances are basic to the execution of techniques. If stances are not assumed correctly and if a karateka cannot change stances rapidly and skillfully, the effectiveness of his or her techniques will be sorely reduced.

TECHNIQUES

Introduction

Techniques include such actions as punches, strikes, kicks, and blocks. While the latter are defensive movements, they may also be used offensively. Similarly, though punches, strikes, and kicks are primarily offensive skills, they are sometimes used defensively to strike an onrushing arm or leg in a parrying action. Besides, in response to being attacked, a good offense frequently results in the best defense.

In this basic publication only hand and foot techniques will be discussed. One should be aware, however, that many parts of the body can be utilized to strike a blow. Figure 5-17 gives some idea of the variety possible as well as some insight into the complexity of karate in general. While, with diligent work, it is possible to acquire considerable proficiency in a relatively short time, one can devote a lifetime to the activity and still not completely master every phase. The statement is not made to discourage participation in karate; in fact, it is hoped that by revealing the lifelong challenge that karate training offers, the opposite will be achieved.

Fig. 5-17.
Some of the variety of areas that can be used to deliver karate blows. Gray areas indicate areas of contact.

A. Head
B. Forefist
C. Hammer fist
D. Thumb knuckle
E. Palm heel
F. Knife-hand
G. Ridge-hand
H. Spear-hand
I. Spear-finger
J. Elbow (up or down)
K. Elbow (back or forward)
L. Knee
M. Edge of foot
N. Instep
O. Heel of foot
P. Ball of foot

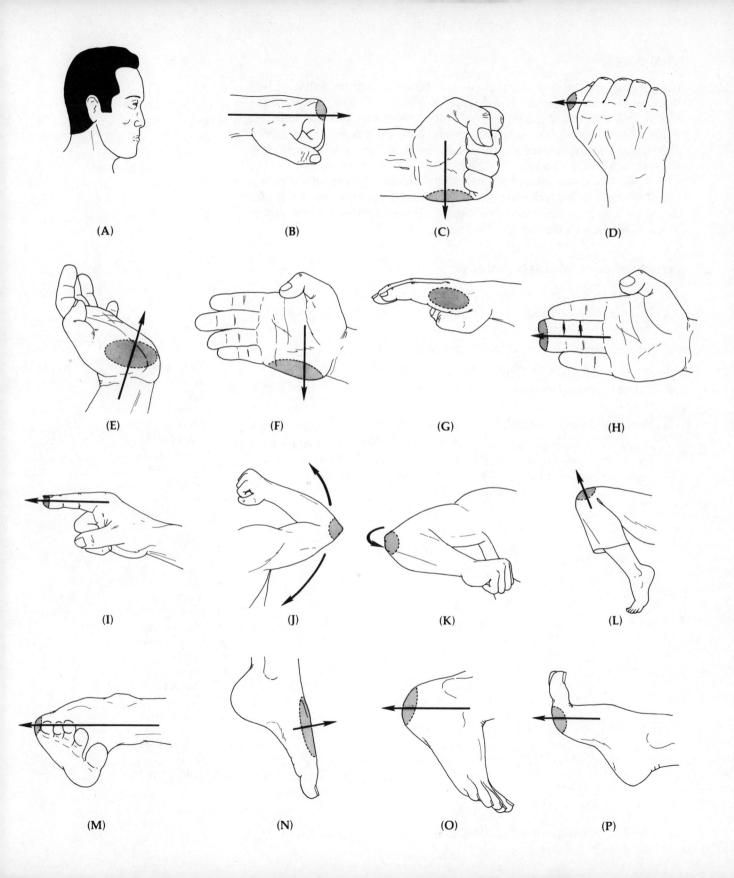

(A)

(B)

(C)

(D)

(E)

(F)

(G)

(H)

(I)

(J)

(K)

(L)

(M)

(N)

(O)

(P)

Vital Points

For greatest effectiveness in actual combat, blows should be delivered to those areas of an opponent's body where they will most likely deter continued attack by causing pain and/or injury. However, because serious injury or even death may result from forceful karate blows, one must exercise restraint *unless* full force is absolutely necessary to save one's life— **Never Use Excessive Force.**

Figure 5-18 shows *some* of the body's vital points. The karateka should visualize them during technique and kata training to get into the habit of aiming at specific targets and not merely delivering blows at random. Knowledge of the vital points must not be abused.

performance points for techniques

1. Always *look* at the intended target before executing any technique.
2. Practice each technique *slowly* until it is mastered; then gradually increase the speed.
3. Do not emphasize speed at the expense of *proper form.*
4. Strive to perform techniques *smoothly, gracefully,* and *forcefully.*
5. Try to maintain *balance* before, during, and after the execution of each technique.
6. *Summate* forces skillfully.
7. Always *withdraw* the arm or leg immediately after executing a technique. This point cannot be stressed enough. Rapid withdrawal prevents the opponent from grabbing the appendage and also permits one to immediately deliver another technique.

Fig. 5-18.
Some of the vital points of the body

1. Bridge of nose
2. Temple
3. Eye
4. Philtrum
5. Chin
6. Side of neck
7. Adam's apple
8. Collar bone
9. Arm pit
10. Solar plexus
11. Front of elbow
12. Ribs
13. Abdomen
14. Testicles
15. Knee
16. Shin
17. Ankle
18. Skull
19. Back of neck
20. Center of back
21. Elbow
22. Wrist
23. Kidneys
24. Coccyx
25. Back of thigh
26. Side of knee
27. Back of knee
28. Instep
29. Achilles tendon

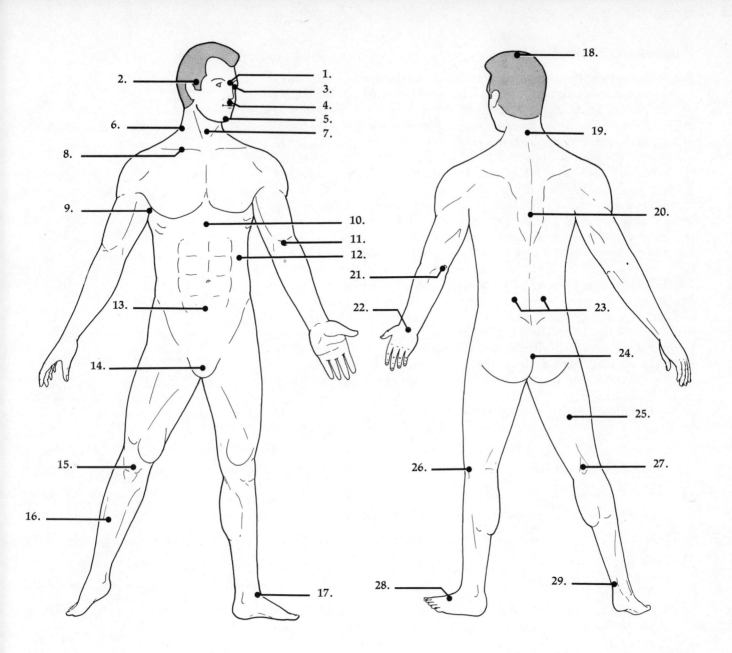

Punches and Strikes

The blows that can be delivered with the hands are divided into two classifications—punches and strikes. Punches refer to blows that involve the fist and are delivered with a considerable amount of body movement, such as the lunge punch (Fig. 5-23). Hand strikes may involve the fist, open hand, or any hand formation, and body motion is comparatively slight. Nearly all the force of the blow is developed through arm movement. Examples include the back fist (Fig. 5-24) and the knife-hand strikes (Figs. 5-26 and 5-27).

There are two ways to make a fist: the most common is similar to a boxer's fist (Fig. 5-19D). The more effective type, the karate fist, is shown in (E). This type of fist decreases the chances for the thumb to catch in an opponent's clothing, is more compact and solid than the boxing-style fist, and is thus able to transmit more force to the target upon contact.

The initial steps in forming both types of fists are identical. Begin with your hand in the open position (A), then forcefully bend the fingers at the first and second joints to form a "half-fist" (B). Next, bend the knuckle joints and roll the fingers into a tightly clenched ball (C). Then to form the boxer's fist press the thumb firmly against the index and middle fingers (D). For the karate fist, bend the joint of the thumb tightly so it can be placed in the "small cup" formed by the index finger (E). In either case, a tightly clenched fist helps protect the finger joints against injury, and by giving greater tension to the wrist helps to protect that also.

Fig. 5-19.
Procedure for forming the two kinds of fists commonly used in karate—boxer style (D) and karate style (E)

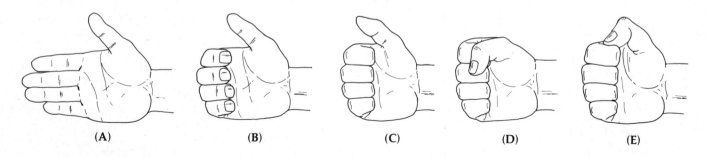

(A)   (B)   (C)   (D)   (E)

Next to the fist, the knife-hand is probably the most used hand formation in karate. It is certainly one of the most versatile, since both the outer and inner edges of the hand (Fig. 5-17 F, G) can be used as striking surfaces. Even the fingertips can be used, in which case the formation is called a "spearhand" (Fig. 5-17H).

In forming the knife-hand (Fig. 5-20), press your fingers closely together and bend them slightly, especially the middle fingers. Some karatekas strive to keep the tips of the three middle fingers in line while others prefer to keep only the tips of the middle and ring fingers in line. Your thumb should be forcefully bent but should not quite touch the hand. The palm of your hand should remain flat and the entire hand, including the fingers and thumb, should be rigidly tensed.

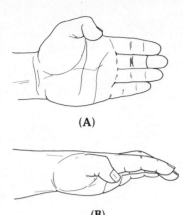

(A)

(B)

Fig. 5-20. Knife-hand

When the inner edge of the hand is used as the striking surface (called a ridge-hand, Fig. 5-17G), your thumb must be bent inward over the palm surface. If the thumb is not tucked inward, it may be injured upon contact.

forefist punch

The forefist punch (Fig. 5-21) is usually the first one taught to a beginning karateka. In the ready stance, the karateka stands with one arm (the left in this illustration) held directly out from the shoulder, the palm facing downward (A). The right fist is positioned at the waist with the palm facing upward. In some karate styles the right fist will be held as high up on the side as possible, near the level of the chest muscles.

From the preparatory position (A) the right fist is thrust directly toward the target. Rotate the wrist 180° so that at the point of contact the palm of the right fist faces downward (C). If the target is above the hip level, the fist should, of course, travel upward as well as forward. Conversely, for groin punches your fist should angle downward. You should practice delivering punches at all levels and with both the right and left hands. While the right arm is extending (B), bring your left arm forcefully back to the waist position (C). This causes the right (punching) shoulder to rotate forward. Also, immediately before the right arm is thrust forward, snap your right hip forward rapidly. Both actions serve to increase the force of the punch.

When practicing the forefist, the punching arm should not be completely extended because injury to the elbow joint might result. In actual combat the arm should not be fully straightened until after contact is made with the target.

Fig. 5-21. Forefist

(A)

(B)

(C)

Although you will begin practicing the forefist from a ready stance as shown in Fig. 5-21, you will seldom employ this method in combat. Because the stance is rather unstable, you would be pushed backward upon contact, thereby diminishing the force of the blow. Therefore whenever the situation permits, keep one foot forward when punching. If the foot *opposite* the punching arm is forward upon contact, the technique is referred to as a reverse punch (Fig. 5-22). If both the arm and foot on the *same side* of the body are forward, the technique is termed a lunge punch (Fig. 5-23).

The reverse and the lunge punches are the most powerful ones in a karateka's repertoire. Basically, three factors account for this: (1) The position in both cases is very stable because of the large base of support. (2) The rigidly straightened rear leg prevents the body from being shoved to the rear when the punch lands (see action-reaction, page 53). (3) Most important, the great force of the punches results from the summation of many forces that are successively developed by a number of muscle groups. A forward step (force #1) preceding the punching action adds immensely to the force of a blow. Immediately after the forward foot touches the floor and while the body is still shifting forward (force #2), the trunk (force #3) and shoulder (force #4) on the punching side rotate forward. As the shoulder nears its most forward position, the punching arm is powerfully extended (force #6), slightly preceded by the drawing back of the opposite arm (force #5). The last force (#7) is obtained by the rotation of the wrist upon contact. If all of these forces are successively and smoothly added, the final total force will be equal to the sum of the seven contributing forces. Considerable practice is necessary, though, to acquire the proper rhythm to achieve the maximum force from a blow. As with all techniques, the lunge

Fig. 5-22. Reverse punch

(D) (C) (B) (A)

and reverse punches must be performed with both the right and left arms, and at all levels—high, middle, and low.

In the initial stages of training, the movement should be practiced very slowly, preferably in front of a mirror to check for proper form. After the proper habit pattern is formed, the karateka should begin increasing speed. Ultimately, one will be able to deliver a series of alternate arm punches with blinding swiftness.

Fig. 5-23. Lunge punch

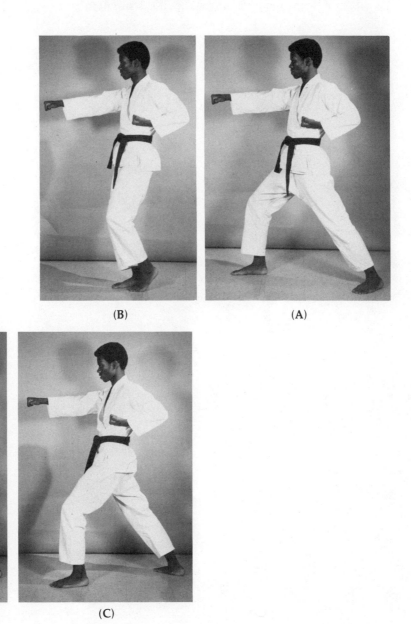

(B)   (A)

(D)   (C)

back fist strike

This technique (Fig. 5-24) is excellent for striking to the sides or even to the rear. To strike to the rear, however, more hip rotation is necessary. Not as much force can be developed when executing the back fist in a forward direction, but the movement is very fast and therefore still useful. Usually, the back fist is delivered from the horse stance or forward stance, but like most techniques it can be thrown from practically any stance if the situation requires it.

(A)

(B)

(C)

(D)

Fig. 5-24. Back fist strike

The starting position for the back fist is from the midchest area (B) with the forearm parallel to the floor. The palm of your fist may face either the floor or your chest. Contract your shoulder muscles to powerfully swing the arm to (C). Then, extend your arm at the elbow joint (D). Once again, for maximal summation of forces the entire sequence of movements must be smooth. Any hesitation reduces the final total force. After impact, return the striking arm *immediately* to the starting position (B). A swift, "snapping" action best describes the entire movement. A karateka always returns to the starting position immediately after a technique is executed to be better prepared to defend himself or to deliver another blow.

If the punch begins with the fist facing the floor as in Fig. 5-25 (A), an additional force is added by the 90° rotation of the wrist near the moment of contact. Also, with the fist in the palm-down position (A), one can deliver the strike without rotating the wrist so that the bottom of the fist (hammer fist, Fig. 5-17 C) makes contact with the target.

inverted fist strike

The inverted fist strike (Fig. 5-25) is merely a variation of the back fist. It is used to attack an opponent's face, especially the bridge of the nose. The starting position (A) is similar to that of the back fist. (Compare Fig. 5-24 C with Fig. 5-25 A). Forces are also generated in the same way. However, instead of the forearm remaining parallel to the floor, it is rotated upward and to the side (B), and then downward (C) to the target. Like the back fist, this strike can also be executed to the front. In such cases, rotate your hips and shoulders in the direction of the strike when the stance permits. The movement of the hips should be slight but extremely fast.

Fig. 5-25. Inverted fist strike

(C)   (B)   (A)

One can deliver a more forceful punch with the inverted fist than with the back fist because it travels a greater distance. The less direct a line is from its starting point to impact, the slower the delivery time.

outside knife-hand strike

Knife-hand strikes (Fig. 5-26), due to their chopping action, are often called karate chops by laymen. Usually, they are delivered from a horse, forward, or sanchin stance. The outside knife-hand strike begins with the striking hand in a knife-hand form and near the ear on the same side of the body (A). Note that the palm faces away from the head, with the thumb knuckle pointing towards the floor and the elbow pointing to the rear and side. Because a number of muscle groups are involved, force upon impact can be ation the karateka has just finished delivering a *left* outside knife-hand strike (A) and is preparing to follow-up with a *right* outside knife-hand. He does not even begin to move his right arm until his right hip has rotated forward (B) to produce force #1. Force #2 is developed by the forward rotation of the shoulder. The right hand is then swung forward in an arching, chopping motion (force #3). If the wrist starts to flex toward the little finger (ulnar flexion) immediately before contact, an additional force is created. The right elbow is never *completely* straightened, not even at the moment of impact (D) when the entire body should be tensed. Here, most beginners tend to forget the abdominal muscles. If they are not forcefully tensed, the upper body is pushed backward upon impact which, of course, reduces the force of the blow.

Fig. 5-26.
Outside knife-hand strike

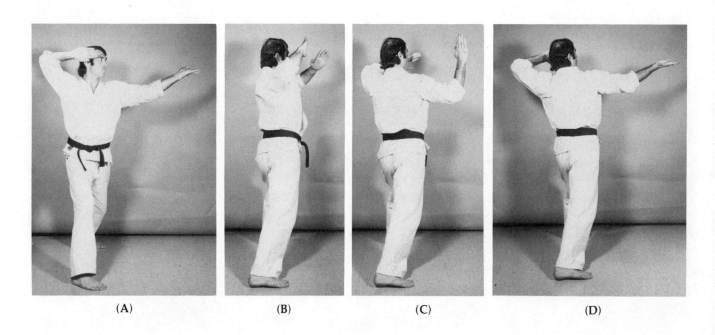

(A)   (B)   (C)   (D)

In (D) the karateka is in perfect position for executing another *left* knife-hand strike because he has brought his left arm straight back into the correct preparatory position. This movement also has defensive value since it protects the left side of his head. During practice, one is often taught to bring the opposing hand back to the hip as if in preparation for executing a forefist punch. (Refer to Fig. 5-21.) Of course, there is no single correct movement for the left hand because so much depends on the situation, especially in sparring or combat. In any case, a karateka should practice a series of left and right knife-hand strikes beginning with slow movements and slowly increasing the speed until he or she can perform them with lightning swiftness.

Fig. 5-27.
Inside knife-hand strike

(D)

inside knife-hand strike

In Fig. 5-27 (A) the karateka has just delivered a *left* inside knife-hand strike and has already turned his head to the right in preparation for a *right* knife-hand strike. The striking hand is brought near his left ear with the palm facing the head. As with the outside strike, the forces for the blow are generated by the rotation of the hips and shoulders, the chopping action of the striking arm, wrist rotation, and the last-minute ulnar flexion of the wrist.

The outside and inside knife-hand strikes are usually directed toward the head, but they can also be used to strike the lower parts of the body. Both strikes can also be modified somewhat to result in a downward chopping action which is often used against an opponent's collar bone.

(C)

(B)

(A)

Kicks

When properly executed, kicks are the most effective type of blow one can deliver. This is because leg muscles are many times stronger than arm muscles. In addition to strength, legs are longer than arms. Thus by kicking you can reach further to land more powerful blows while simultaneously protecting your vital points from an opponent's blows.

Due to these advantages, a highly skilled karateka will normally deliver more kicks than punches. However, kicks do have disadvantages. In the first place, they are *relatively* slow. Second, because only one foot remains on the floor, one's base of support is quite small. Coupled with the fact that the karateka's center of gravity will nearly always be high, the kicking position is very unstable and the karateka can be pushed off balance easily upon making contact. While the disadvantages of kicking cannot be eliminated, their effects can be reduced by close adherence to the performance points listed below.

The fundamental factor is *balance*. To remain in a balanced state before, during, and after a kick, your center of gravity must fall within the base of support (Fig. 5-28). If the center of gravity falls too near the heel boundary (A) you will be pushed backward and off balance when your kicking foot hits the target (see front kick, Fig. 5-29 D). On the other hand, if the center of gravity is too far forward (C) you will lose balance in a forward direction if you miss the target. The latter, of course, unnecessarily exposes you to a counter-attack and prevents the quick return of the kicking foot to a preparatory position (Fig. 5-29 B) for another kick. As a rule, it is most sensible to keep your center of gravity directly over the center of the base of support (B).

The performance techniques for kicks are the same as those previously stated on page 74. For emphasis, the most significant of those are again listed here along with a few that apply solely to kicks.

1. *Look* at the opponent before starting a kick and keep him in view throughout the kick.
2. *Summate* forces effectively.
3. Although there is often a tendency for the heel of the supporting foot to lift, keep the *entire* foot on the floor for greater stability.
4. Keep the body's center of gravity directly in the *center* of the base of support to maintain balance.
5. *Immediately* withdraw the striking foot after impact to keep your opponent from grabbing it.

Fig. 5-28.
During a kick, one's center of gravity should fall in the center of the supporting foot.

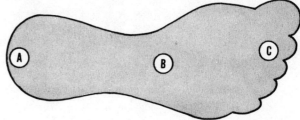

front snap kick

As with all techniques, the front snap kick should be practiced from both sides of the body. It also can be executed from practically any stance, but the beginner is usually first taught to deliver it from the forward stance as shown in Fig. 5-29.

Fig. 5-29. Front snap kick

(A)   (B)   (C)   (D)

When the body's forces are properly summated, force #1 is produced by the forward movement of the body's center of gravity so that it lies over the left foot (B). Almost simultaneously, the knee of the right leg drives upward (force #2) so that a line from the hip joint to the knee points directly at the target. Obviously for kicks to the jaw, chest, or even stomach, the knee must be raised higher than for kicks to an opponent's knee or groin. Just before the knee reaches its highest point the lower leg is forcefully swung forward (force #3) and immediately brought back to position (B). The entire movement of the lower leg has a *snapping* action. Before the kicking leg is brought back to assume another forward stance (A), it hesitates for a moment at (B) in preparation for another front snap kick. Perfect balance must be maintained throughout the execution of this technique. For variety, one may step forward with the right foot from (B) to a right forward stance and then deliver a *left* front snap kick.

Throughout the entire kick (A–D) the upper body should be in a vertical posture. For high kicks this is difficult, or even impossible, unless one has developed considerable flexibility. The supporting foot must remain completely in contact with the floor. If the heel is permitted to rise, one's base is reduced and his or her stability, which is rather tenuous anyway, is further diminished.

Usually, the toes of the striking foot are drawn upward and back so that the ball of the foot makes contact with the target (Fig. 5-17 P). For kicks to an opponent's groin, though, the instep of the foot should be used, as shown in Fig. 5-17 N.

front thrust kick

The front thrust kick (Fig. 5-30) is similar to the snap kick. However, it is used when the target is a bit farther away from the karateka. The only difference in execution is that the lower leg is not so much snapped as it is *thrust* forward from (C). Because the attacking leg extends farther to the front, one has to lean a bit back (D) with the upper body to keep the center of gravity over the supporting foot and thus maintain equilibrium.

Fig. 5-30. Front thrust kick

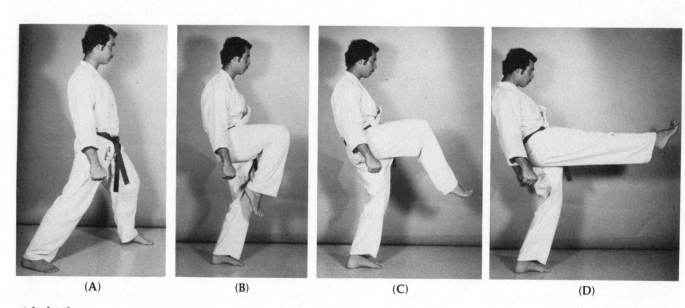

(A)   (B)   (C)   (D)

side kicks

For most karatekas, side kicks are the most frequently employed foot blows. As the name indicates, this kick is executed to the sides. It can be directed at any level, but because of balance and flexibility limitations, the beginner is advised to begin by practicing low side kicks (knee level or lower). If the karateka works on the stretching exercises, especially on the chinese splits, he or she will quickly develop the flexibility required to execute the middle side kicks (stomach level) shown in Fig. 5-31, and with perseverance will eventually work up to the high side kicks (Fig. 5-32). Side kicks are most commonly executed from the horse stance but can be performed from virtually any stance. In every case, however, the kicking leg must first pass through the crane stance shown in Fig. 5-32 (B). To execute a side kick from the forward stance the rear foot is normally brought forward to become the kicking foot.

To begin the kick, shift your weight to the supporting leg and bring the kicking foot up to the inner knee joint of the supporting leg. In the early stages of learning, hesitate for a moment in the crane stance before driving the kicking foot in a *straight line* toward the target. As proficiency increases, gradually eliminate the hesitation so that the two actions flow into one smooth, continuous motion. There can be no shortcuts in this technique; the kicking foot must *pass through* the crane stance for maximal kicking force. Note that the toes of the kicking foot are drawn up and the heel is forcefully extended so that the foot will be absolutely rigid upon contact (see action-reaction, page 53). The outer edge of the foot also juts outward (D) into the foot edge form depicted in Fig. 5-17M.

Fig. 5-31. Middle side kick

(D)   (C)   (B)   (A)

Fig. 5-32. High side kick

(A)   (B)   (C)   (D)

The force for the kick is developed by lifting your kicking knee upward (Fig. 5-32 C), straightening the supporting leg (from B to C), pivoting on the supporting foot (B to C), and then extending the kicking leg (D). Hold your upper body as erect as possible. Naturally, the higher you kick, the more you are forced to lean to the side. It also follows that for high kicks the kicking knee must be lifted higher before the leg is extended to strike the target. Compare Fig. 5-31 (B) with Fig. 5-32 (C).

Like the front kick, the side kick may be delivered with either a snapping or thrusting action. The latter is used when a greater range is required, and because the foot travels over a greater distance, more force can be generated with a thrust. To maintain balance, the thrusting movement requires quite a bit more body lean than is used with a snap kick. The pivoting of the supporting foot, shown most clearly in Fig. 5-31 (C and D) and Fig. 5-32 (B and C), is also very helpful in increasing stability so a more forceful kick can be delivered. The supporting foot must be firmly planted on the floor when impact occurs.

After the kick is delivered, the foot must *immediately* be brought back to the crane stance (Fig. 5-32B) and held in that position briefly before being placed back on the floor. By hesitating, the karateka remains in position to rapidly execute another side kick if the situation warrants.

roundhouse kick

The roundhouse kick does not travel in a straight line to the target but takes a circular path. As a result it takes a bit more time to deliver than the previously discussed kicks, but by traveling a greater distance more force is developed.

The greatest concentration of force is developed when the roundhouse kick is performed from a forward stance (Fig. 5-33 A). Considerable force is generated merely by shifting your body weight forward onto the supporting foot (B) which allows the left hip to rotate much further forward (B and C). Without the foot pivot, hip rotation is severely limited and much of the kick's force is lost. As the hips near full rotation, lift the knee of the kicking foot upward and a bit forward (C). Because the left knee is bent, the kicking knee can swing forward much more rapidly than if it were straight. Also from the bent position (C) the left lower leg can be *whipped* forward in a *circular* path, a movement which results in great force upon impact (D).

The roundhouse kick is normally directed toward an opponent's head. At contact the foot is usually extended (D) with the *instep* of the foot being the striking surface (see Fig. 5-17 N). Sometimes the toes are flexed toward the knee, however, so the ball of the foot makes contact (see Fig. 5-17 P).

Although the *supporting* leg may be bent during the delivery of the kick, it should be straightened before impact. For greatest stability, under the circumstances, the heel of the supporting foot must not be lifted from the floor.

When in-fighting, the kicking leg may not even be extended. If an opponent steps toward the karateka just as he or she is delivering the roundhouse kick, the lower part of the kicking leg should not be snapped forward, in which case the attacker is struck with the knee in a vital point such as the ribs, solar plexus, or groin.

Fig. 5-33. Roundhouse kick

(A)

(B)

(C)

(D)

hook kick

Although the hook kick (Fig. 5-34) is one of the more difficult kicks to learn, the beginner will oftentimes execute it by mistake when attempting to deliver a high side kick. In fact, the easiest way to learn the hook movement is to aim a side kick about a foot to the side of the intended target (C), and then swiftly flex the leg at the knee joint to "snap" the heel into the target (D). In combat if a side kick is missed, the karateka will sometimes snap the kicking foot into a hook kick if the opponent is in a vulnerable position.

The hook kick is most commonly performed from a horse stance and is delivered primarily to the head, although it can also be used to attack the groin area. To begin the kick, shift the center of gravity over the supporting leg. At the same time, bring the knee of the kicking leg upward (B). As in the side kick, the kicking leg must pass through the crane stance. By bringing the leg *close* to your chest, you can subsequently drive it over a greater distance and thereby generate a greater force at impact. Extend the left leg (B to C) so as to direct the foot in a *straight* line. *Immediately* after the kicking leg reaches full extension (C), flex it backward with a "snapping" action so the *heel* of the kicking foot makes contact with the target (D). Not as much force can be developed with a hook kick as with a roundhouse kick because the degree of force depends solely on the contraction of one muscle group, the hamstring muscles, located in the rear of the thigh. Due to its deceptiveness, however, this kick can be quite useful.

In the recovery phase of the hook kick, continue from (D) to the position shown in (B). Then, with a brief hesitation, place your left foot back in the horse stance (A) in preparation for a stance change or the execution of another technique.

Fig. 5-34. Hook kick

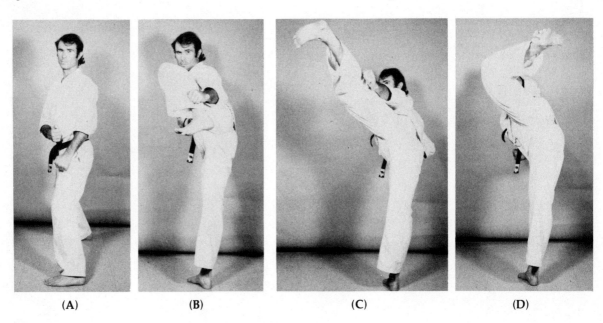

(A)   (B)   (C)   (D)

back kick

The previously discussed kicks are effective against either a frontal or side attack. When one is being attacked from behind, the back kick (Fig. 5-35) is used. It can be delivered from practically any stance as long as the striking leg passes through position (B) and is generally employed to strike an opponent in the area between the solar plexus and the knees. For higher kicks the knee should pass through position (C). Contact is made with the heel of the foot (see Fig. 5-17 O). A variation of the back kick, called the stamping kick (Fig. 5-36), is directed toward the instep of an opponent who is grabbing the karateka from behind.

Fig. 5-35. Back kick

(A) (B) (C) (D)

As with all kicks, you must first look at your target (A), and simultaneously shift your weight to the supporting leg while drawing the knee of the kicking leg forward to (B). Then, with a rebounding action, drive the left leg to the rear. As the leg reaches (C) extend it forcefully and directly toward the target (D). In the case of low back kicks a snapping action is normally the most effective; however, for middle level blows a thrusting action is usually required. Of course, with the latter, you will have to lean your upper body quite a bit forward (D) to keep the center of gravity over the supporting leg to maintain balance. Note that the karateka's body is turned to the side somewhat so he can view the target (D).

In returning the kicking leg to a stance, it first must pass through position (B). It hesitates there for a brief moment in preparation for another back kick.

(A) (B) (C)

Fig. 5-36. Stamping kick

Blocks

Blocks are defensive techniques. The best defense, of course, is to avoid situations where violence is likely to occur. Unfortunately, one is not always able to avoid combat in spite of all efforts. Then one's defense depends upon dodging maneuvers and blocking techniques. Both of these defensive techniques rely on one's skill to rapidly change stances (see page 67). After an opponent makes a physically aggressive move, the karateka should block the blow and swiftly retaliate with an offensive technique to end the encounter.

As with offensive measures, practically any part of the body can be used to block (stop or deflect) an opponent's blow to prevent it from reaching a vital point. Most blocking techniques involve the use of the hands and the karateka should master these before progressing to other techniques.

Performance points for executing blocks are listed below. Some are similar to those for offensive techniques while others are unique to blocking actions.

1. *Look* in the direction of the approaching blow so the block can be accurately applied.

2. Execute the block *forcefully*, even though the usual objective is not to stop the blow but to DEFLECT it.

3. When possible, use the blocking hand on the *same side* of the body as the forward foot. For instance, if the right foot is forward the block should be executed by the right arm and hand.

4. *Tense* entire body at the moment of impact so the force of the block will not be reduced.

5. Maintain body *balance* so follow-up actions can be made more rapidly and skillfully.

6. Immediately after the block makes contact, *withdraw* the blocking hand to put it in position for delivering the next technique and to prevent the opponent from grabbing it.

7. Be prepared to follow a block with an *immediate* offensive action.

8. In blocking, your hands may begin from any point. The initial positions shown in the photographs are merely examples. Still, the blocking hand itself, for greatest effectiveness, must conform to the prescribed patterns of movement.

low block

The low block is used to fend off blows to the abdomen and groin. It can be executed from practically any stance but is most commonly employed from a forward or horse stance. Depending upon which arm or leg an opponent is attacking with, the low block may deflect it to either the inside or outside.

The blocking surface of the arm may be the forearm, knifehand (Fig. 5-17 F), or hammer fist (Fig. 5-17C).

Figure 5-37 shows the execution of a right low block with the hand forming a fist just before impact. At the beginning, the left hand can be in a variety of positions, but here it is in a left low block position with the hand formed into a knife-hand (A). To start the right low block bring the right hand up to the opposite side of the head in the knife-hand position with the palm facing the left ear (A). From this position bring it directly to the low block position shown in (D). Note that the arm is parallel to the right thigh.

Considerable force may have to be developed to block a blow, especially if one is defending against a kick. The initial force in the summation of forces is produced by the shoulder muscles bringing the upper right arm toward the side (from A). From this position, extend the arm at the elbow joint (B). As the right hand nears the point of impact it is formed into a fist (C) or knife-hand and rotates to (D) to add a bit to the final force. The elbow joint of the blocking arm should be bent inward at about an angle of twenty degrees upon contact with the attacking limb.

While the right arm is executing a low block, the left arm is simultaneously brought back to the waist (D) in preparation for a reverse or lunge punch. This drawing back action also results in a more forceful block. For practice one should step forward with the left foot and execute a left low block.

Fig. 5-37. Low block

(A)

(D)

(C)

(B)

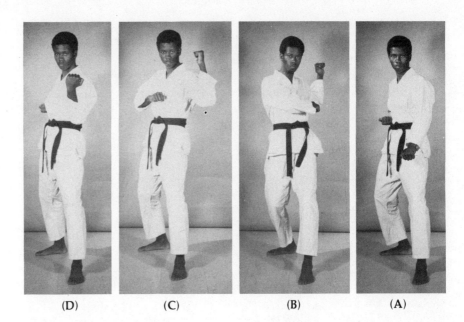

Fig. 5-38. Middle outside block

(D)   (C)   (B)   (A)

middle outside block

Also referred to as an outside forearm block, the middle outside technique is employed to protect one's neck, solar plexus, ribs, and upper abdomen. This technique is called an *outside* block because the action begins from an outside position (B) and is usually used to strike the *outer* surface of an attacking limb.

In Fig. 5-38 the left arm is used to demonstrate the middle outside block. If an opponent attacks with either the right arm or leg, the blocking arm will strike the outer surface and deflect it inward. As a result the opponent will be out of position to strike with either the left hand or foot. This block *can* be used to parry a blow being delivered by an opponent's left arm or leg. In such cases the inner surface of the attacker's limb will be struck. This inner technique can be effective when employed by an expert karate artist if he or she follows immediately with an offensive strike. The beginner, however, is not advised to use this technique.

Initially, put your blocking arm and hand in position to deliver the block; that is, draw your left hand near the left ear (B). By having your palm facing forward, you can subsequently rotate your wrist to the position shown in (D) to add its force to the impact. Note that the karateka has also rotated his left hip rearward (B) before starting the block. Actually, the movement is somewhat exaggerated in this photograph for illustrative purposes. Body movements for the proper summation of forces begin with forward rotation of the left hip, followed by rotation of the trunk and shoulders (C). Then, contract the left chest muscles powerfully to swing your arm to (D). At the same time, draw the right fist back forcefully from (C) to (D); this helps increase the speed of the upper body's rotation. *Immediately* before contact is made, rotate the left wrist forcefully so the palm faces your face. At impact, the angle of the elbow joint should be a little more than ninety degrees. Contact may be made with the forearm, the bottom of the fist (hammer hand), or with a knife-hand.

Like all techniques, you should practice this block with both arms. Blocks should be executed from both sides with equal swiftness, force, and accuracy.

middle inside block

Like the outside block, the middle inside block is used to parry blows to the upper part of the body. It can also be executed a bit higher than normal to defend against blows to the face. The technique is termed an *inside* block because the action begins from an inside position (B) and is generally employed to strike the *inner* surface of an attacking limb.

In Fig. 5-39 the karateka is using his left arm to demonstrate this block. The right arm may be in practically any position at the start of the block. However, since the block often follows a forefist punch, the right arm is shown in that position (A). The middle inside block with the left arm is usually used to deflect a blow being delivered by an opponent's right arm or leg. It is especially effective since the block normally leaves the opponent exposed to a frontal attack. Though highly skilled karateka may on occasion have to use this block in defense against a left-handed attack, a beginner is advised not to use it for such purposes.

In starting the middle inside block, first bring your left arm across the front of the body. This movement results in more force being developed in a sidewards direction as you powerfully swing your forearm back to the left

Fig. 5-39. Middle inside block

(A)   (B)

side of the body. If the left arm were swung directly from (A) to (D), very little sideward force could be generated to parry a blow. After the left shoulder muscles contract powerfully to bring the arm from (B) to (C), rotate the forearm strongly to (D). This rotation is a key point in the technique and occurs with the elbow acting as the fulcrum. Note in (C) and (D), that the elbow remains in essentially the same spot. The final force in the summation of forces is added by the 90° rotation of the left wrist from (B) to (D). It is difficult to demonstrate the rotation of the wrist in the photographs, but this is what must occur for the technique to be most effective. If the wrist did not rotate, the thumb knuckle of the fist would point toward the karateka's face in (D) instead of to the side. As with most hand blocks, the left hand can be formed into either a fist or a knife-hand (or ridge-hand, Fig. 5-17G).

At the conclusion of both inside and outside middle blocks, the elbow joint should be bent at about 90°. However, the forearm must *not* be vertical to the floor in either case. More accurately, it should *not* be perpendicular to the attacking limb upon impact. In both Fig. 5-38 (D) and Fig. 5-39 (D) the blocking forearm, as well as the upper arm, is held at roughly 45° to the floor.

While the left arm is executing the block, the right arm is being withdrawn, and it can assume any punching or striking position. Everything depends upon the combative situation, but withdrawing the right fist to a position in preparation for a forefist punch is good practice for the beginner. Note that the blocking arm passes on the *outside* of the right arm. From (C) to (D), the withdrawing movement of the right arm is forceful to help make the left shoulder rotate forward more rapidly.

(C)

(D)

high block

The high block is employed to protect the head against downward blows or to cause blows directed toward the face to be deflected upward. Although this particular block can be performed from any stance, it can be more forcefully executed from a forward or horse stance.

In Fig. 5-40 the right hand is used to execute the high block. Note that the leg on the same side of the body is forward. Whenever feasible, this should be the case when performing any block. The position of the hands at the beginning of the technique is not necessarily the position shown in (A). For example, the block may start from the positions depicted in Fig. 5-38 (A) and Fig. 5-39 (A), or from any number of other positions.

Since the force for the block is developed almost exclusively by the right shoulder muscles they must contract very powerfully to *swing* the arm to (D). At the moment of impact the karateka's upper body should be directly facing the opponent with his or her back erect. In addition, the blocking forearm should be slightly in front of, and about two and a half inches from, the forehead. It is also important for the forearm *not* to be parallel to the floor but at an angle upward. As mentioned previously, the attacking arm must be prevented from perpendicularly striking the blocking surface. The elbow joint should be flexed at about a 100° angle. The palm of the right fist faces forward (D) so that the outer surface of the forearm will receive the attacking blow. Although the bony ridge of the wrist is the usual point of contact, a knife-hand or hammer fist (Fig. 5-17C) can also be used.

In Fig. 5-40, while the block is being executed, the left arm slides along the inside of the blocking arm and is brought back to the side in preparation for delivery of a punch or another block. If the hands are held in the ready position as shown in Fig. 5-41, the arms will not necessarily cross. One arm will execute the block and the other may be brought straight back to the side. It is impossible to illustrate or discuss every possibility for executing the high block, but one should realize that the movements will not always begin as shown in Fig. 5-41 (A). What does remain constant, however, is the basic movement of the blocking arm.

Fig. 5-40. High block

(A) (B)

(C) (D)

high X-block

Like the high block, the high X-block (Fig. 5-41) is used to defend oneself against downward blows to the head, or to deflect blows toward the face in an upward direction. It is a fast block that is particularly effective against a pole attack or powerful hand attacks. Since less strength is required in this technique, a relatively weak person will sometimes find it necessary to utilize the "X" technique instead of the high block. Because it leaves the defender vulnerable to a counter attack, it is not a good idea to rely on the X-block too often.

In executing, contract the muscles of *both* shoulders forcefully to bring the arms upward. This makes this block twice as strong as a single-arm high block. For right-handed people, the *right* arm normally passes on the inside of the left arm. At this point just as the arms touch (B), they will form a cradle. This junction contacts the underside of an advancing punch to deflect it upward. As the blocking arms continue upward, thrust the elbows upward and extend the arms at the elbow joint to form an angle of about 135°. Do not extend the elbows to the sides beyond the shoulders since this weakens the block. Although the forearms are rather close to the karateka's body in (B), by the time they reach (D) they are about nine inches in front of the forehead and a bit above his head. At (D) the palms of the fist face downward and slightly outward. Although the hands are formed into fists in this illustration, they may also be in the knife-hand position. One advantage of the knife-hand position is that the hands can rotate, palms forward, and grasp the opponent's hand during the block.

Fig. 5-41. High X-block

(A) (B) (C) (D)

Fig. 5-42. Low X-block

(A)   (B)   (C)

low X-block

The low X-block is employed to protect the groin from kicking attacks or low punches. It can be executed from practically any stance but is most often used from a forward, horse, or X-stance. The latter, shown in Fig. 5-13 (C and D) helps to further protect the genitals.

Before delivering the low X-block, the karateka in Fig. 5-42 may prefer to simultaneously raise his arms and straighten his legs slightly (B). Because the arms subsequently cover a greater distance to (C), greater force can be developed with the block. If speed is of greatest importance, however, one should thrust downward from (A). For right-handed people, the right arm normally passes to the outside of the left arm to form a cradle. This junction contacts the upperside of the attacking limb and forces it downward. Upon impact, the arms must be touching (C), and the fists should continue downward. Note that the arms are almost fully extended. During the block, the chest muscles should contract powerfully.

The palms of the fist face upward and slightly inward (C); however, one's hands may also be in the knife-hand form so they can rotate downward to grasp the opponent's leg during the block.

Balance is the essential ingredient in this technique. By leaning the upper body slightly forward, but still keeping it straight, one's stability is increased. This lean is especially important when the karateka is in the horse stance, because stability in the backward direction is then not nearly as good as with the forward stance.

After executing the low X-block, one must be prepared to immediately assume the attack, preferably using kicking techniques.

knife-hand block

The knife-hand block is used to parry attacks to one's chest, neck, or head. As in Fig. 5-43, the block is commonly delivered from a back stance, although cat and forward stances are often used, too. Some karateka assume the blocking position (D) as a ready posture for sparring and actual combat.

Using the left hand to demonstrate the block in Fig. 5-43, the karateka has initiated the movement from the knife-hand position shown in (D). His left hand remains in a knife-hand form as it is brought across the body to the right side of the neck. In a circular motion, with the elbow acting as the fulcrum, the hand continues forward and downward to execute the block. Considerable force is generated due to the distance the left hand must travel. Additional force is added by the 180° wrist rotation from (C) to (D). The effectiveness of the block is further intensified due to the small area of contact of the knife-hand (see Fig. 5-17 F). In fact, the block is often used to break the bones in the forearm of the attacking arm.

In (D), the right hand is in position to deliver a spear hand thrust (Fig. 5-17 H) or a forefist punch. As always, it must be kept in mind that there is no specific initial position required for either hand. Its initial position depends on the combative situation. However, the movement of the blocking hand, as described here, must be strictly followed for greatest effectiveness.

Fig. 5-43. Knife-hand block

(A)   (B)

(C)   (D)

6 SPARRING AND SELF-DEFENSE

Although many people practice karate strictly as a form of exercise or for a satisfying kinesthetic experience, most wish to obtain self-defense benefits. Since this ability is based on the standard stances and techniques, all who participate in karate, no matter what their personal objectives are, improve their self-defense capabilities to some extent. In other words, by mastering the fundamental skills one instinctively delivers blows rapidly and forcefully. But there is more to fighting than merely delivering blows. To most effectively prepare oneself for fighting, one must practice against an opponent. Of course all-out combat cannot be permitted since serious injuries would result. Training must, therefore, consist of mock fighting situations called *sparring*.

The most effective type of sparring is called freestyle sparring. It is identical to actual combat except that players do not make forceful contact. Techniques are delivered with full force and speed but they barely touch the opponent. Because superb control is required, a karateka can never be expected to progress directly from basic skill training to free-style sparring. The trainee must first successfully pass through several intermediate stages, each of which more closely approaches freestyle.

PREARRANGED SPARRING

The safest and most sensible way to introduce karate players to sparring is with a *prearranged* pattern of blows and blocks with both participants knowing exactly what techniques are to be used. Initial patterns should be very simple, with complexity increasing as proficiency is gained. There are a wide variety of patterns in prearranged sparring that can and should be practiced; patterns should, of course, be arranged according to one's personal needs. For instance, if the karateka has difficulty in defending against kicks, the opponent should stress kicking techniques. Each sparring pattern should be executed *slowly* at first, and then gradually worked up to much faster speeds.

In prearranged sparring, one contestant is assigned the role of *attacker* and the other the role of *defender*. The *attacker* always makes the first move, an offensive technique such as a punch or kick. The *defender's* first move will be to block the blow and immediately follow with one or more offensive techniques. In more complex patterns, the *attacker* will deliver more than one blow. The *defender* will block each of them and will always end the pattern with one or more offensive techniques. The reason for this is that the *defender* must not only block the attacker's blows, but must prevent continued aggression by delivering a crippling strike.

Typical Procedures

A precise procedure must be followed so both contestants will be completely prepared for the action. Although there may be slight variations between schools, a typical procedure follows:

1. Opponents face each other at a distance of about two and one-half feet. Each assumes a ready stance and bows toward the other (Fig. 2-8).

2. The instructor asks, "Ready?"

3. The contestants answer, "Yes," if they know the pattern and are prepared to begin. Then each assumes the fighting stance of his choice (for an example, see Fig. 6-1A).

4. After the instructor's command, "Start!," the attacking player leads with an offensive technique and the rest of the movements follow.

5. Immediately after the entire pattern has been completed, the instructor commands, "Stop!" and the players return to their ready stances and again bow to each other.

Principles

During prearranged sparring the players should be guided by the following principles:

1. Each player keeps his or her eyes fixed on the other during the entire pattern as well as during the ceremonial bowing. Some karatekas look at the opponent's eyes, while others prefer keeping their eyes fixed on the opponent's neck or chest. Each player should experiment and find out what personally works best.

2. Punches and kicks fall short of contact or barely touch the opponent.

3. Blocks are executed rapidly and forcefully to prevent offensive techniques from striking the target.

4. Whenever possible blocks should *deflect* rather than stop a blow.

5. The *defender* should deliver the counter-attack immediately *after* executing the last block.

6. Attacking and defending roles should alternate between players.

7. Sparring patterns should begin first from one side of the body, then the other.

Examples of Prearranged Sparring

Thirteen examples of prearranged sparring are shown. These specifically are suggested because they progress logically from simple to complex patterns and provide practice for a variety of stances, foot movements, and techniques. Again, players are advised to *create* patterns which meet their individual needs.

Fig. 6-1.
In (A) the players have assumed the horse stance as their fighting stances. The offensive player begins the sparring with a *reverse punch* to the face. The defender executes a *high block* and follows with a *reverse punch* to the solar plexus.

(A)

(B)

(C)

(D)

Fig. 6-2.
The pattern in this illustration is the same as that shown in the previous one, however, it is more advanced and realistic in that the *high block* deflects the aggressor's punch as it is being delivered (B). It is best to begin a pattern as simply as possible and slowly increase the speed to a maximal level.

(A)

(B)

(C)

Fig. 6-3.
From his fighting stance, the aggressor delivers a *front snap kick*. The defender diverts the blow with a *low block* (B) and pivots to deliver a *reverse punch* (C). Rapid, forceful hip rotation is the basis for a powerful blow. The defender will initially execute his block and punch in two very distinct movements. Eventually these movements will be performed almost simultaneously.

(A)

(B)

(C)

Fig. 6-4.
From the fighting stance shown in Fig. 6-3, the offensive player delivers a *reverse punch* to the face. The defender deflects it with a *high block* (A) and follows with his own *reverse punch*. Then, he drives his knee (gently, very gently) to the groin area or abdomen. He can increase the force of the blow by grabbing the opponent's gi (C). As always, in the interests of safety, the pattern must be performed slowly at first.

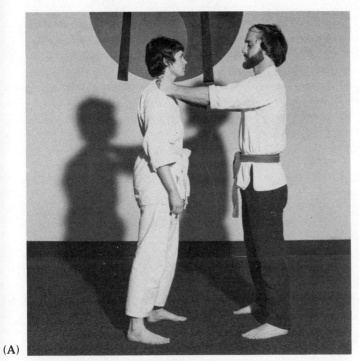

(A)

(B)

(C)

Fig. 6-5.

When the attacker grabs his victim by the shoulders, she steps back while driving her arms upward (B). Normally, the aggressor's grip will be broken as he is pulled forward. The girl immediately steps forward, grasps the attacker's shoulders, and drives her *knee* into his groin (C). If rape was on his mind, this blow will cause his desire for a sexual encounter to diminish rather swiftly. To break a single hand choke, the girl should use a *high block* technique while stepping to the rear (B).

(A)

(B)

(C)

Fig. 6-6.
Having been rebuked (in the previous illustration), the attacker wisely seeks gentler prey and decides to vary his technique. This time he grabs his intended victim from the side. The girl quickly shifts her body away from him (B) which tends to draw him toward her. The movement also diverts the man's attention from her *side kick*. Then, she pivots to a *front stance* and delivers an *elbow strike* to his face (C). In practice, be very careful with the *side kick*, since the knee can easily be seriously injured.

(A)

(B)

(C)

Fig. 6-7.
From a modified *horse stance* (A), the offensive player pivots to a *front stance* and delivers a left *reverse punch* (B). The defender deflects it with a rather high *middle inside block*. Initially, the defender will hesitate at (B) before executing the *knife-hand strike* (C). With practice, the block and strike merge into one continuous motion.

(A)

(B)

(C)

(D)

Fig. 6-8.
With both players in a *horse stance*, the aggressor delivers a *back fist*. The defender counters with a rather high *middle outside block* (A). Then, he grabs the offensive player's sleeve (B). This keeps the opponent close while the defender slides his right foot forward to get into position for delivering a *roundhouse kick* to the head (or abdomen).

Fig. 6-9.

In self defense, a person will usually block a blow and follow immediately with *more* than one offensive technique. Here, the defender deflects a *reverse punch* (B) with a *middle outside block* and with the same hand strikes with a *back fist* (C). Then, he drives a *reverse punch* to the solar plexus (D). Ultimately, there should be no hesitation between the defender's three techniques.

Fig. 6-10.
This pattern begins with both players in a *horse stance*. The defender deflects a *side kick* with a *low block* (A). Then, he defends against a *back fist* with a *middle outside block* (B). Offensively, he drives an *elbow strike* to the solar plexus (C) and snaps a *back fist* to the jaw (D). The defender will often have to execute his blocks while retreating.

Fig. 6-11.

From a *horse stance* (A) the aggressor steps forward and delivers a *lunge punch* at face level. The defender deflects the blow with a *middle inside block* (B). Then, when the aggressor follows with a *reverse punch* to the abdomen, the defender counters with a *low block* (C) and ends the pattern with a *side kick* to the solar plexus (D).

(A)

(B)

(C)

(D)

Fig. 6-12.
This pattern helps one to practice delivering two kicks in succession. The defender diverts a back fist with a *middle outside block* and drives a *side kick* to the ribs. The kick is diverted with a *low block* so while balancing on one foot he delivers a *roundhouse kick* (C). He may then step either behind or in front of the aggressor to execute a *back fist* strike (D).

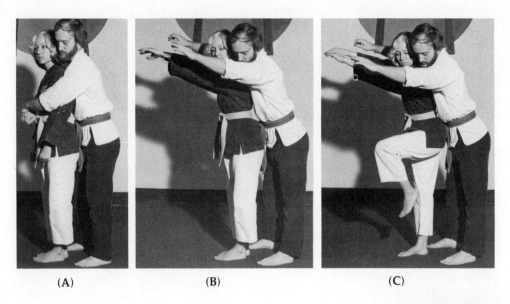

(A)　　　　　　　(B)　　　　　　　(C)

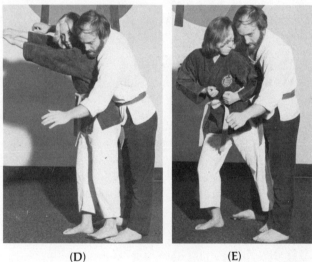

(D)　　　　　　　(E)

Fig. 6-13.
When the attacker grabs his victim from behind (A), she forcefully lifts her arms upward while thrusting her hips to the rear. In (B) the girl's hips should be farther back. Immediately after the man's hold is broken she lifts her knee (C) and executes a *stamping kick* to his instep (D). Then, she drives an *elbow strike* to his ribs (E). Because her elbow travels over a long distance, considerable force can be generated. And since the point of the elbow is small, the force is concentrated in a small area so the pressure at contact is great enough to break a rib. One must, therefore, *be careful* in practice.

Semi-Freestyle Sparring

Semi-freestyle sparring is the intermediate stage between prearranged sparring and freestyle. As such, it has elements of both types. The players decide before action begins on the *number* of techniques the *attacker* is going to deliver, but the *defender* will not have foreknowledge of *which* ones will be used. The *defender* will attempt to block the blows and end the pattern by delivering an offensive technique. Naturally, semi-freestyle sparring begins very simply with the *attacker* delivering only one technique and the *defender* blocking it and following with a punch or kick. As a student becomes more competent, the patterns should become more complex and demanding. All blows either fall slightly short of the target or barely make contact.

Freestyle Sparring

Again, freestyle sparring is the same as actual fighting except that combatants do *not* make forceful contact unless protective equipment is worn. There is no predetermined plan and neither player is designated *attacker* or *defender*. As in serious combat, the roles shift back and forth during the match.

While it is *desirable* to have a qualified instructor for all phases of karate training, it is *absolutely imperative* that one be present and closely involved during freestyle training. The necessity of a capable instructor cannot be sufficiently stressed. Besides controlling and officiating the match, the instructor is the only person who can reliably determine if the contestants are ready for this advanced activity in the first place. Only by observing their behavior over a long period of time can he tell if they have acquired the necessary physical skill and proper spiritual and emotional stability that ultimately permits responsible action.

Since even the most highly qualified instructor may make the wrong decision in allowing a student to spar, it is his responsibility to stay close to the action during matches, especially those between beginners. If a participant does not exhibit sufficient control, the instructor has not only the authority but also the duty to stop the match and keep the player from sparring again until he or she has improved in terms of either skill or attitude.

One can assume any desired stance when the sparring begins; each karateka naturally has individual preferences. Although most competitors prefer the horse stance (Fig. 5-3), others favor the sanchin stance (Fig. 5-8) because it better protects the groin, and still another group uses the cat stance (Fig. 5-6) as their basic fighting stance.

The hand positions can also vary, though again, each karateka soon selects the one he finds most comfortable and effective. To help prevent injury to the hands and fingers, it is best for a beginner to begin freestyle sparring with the hands clenched into fists. As one gains experience, he will probably prefer the knife-hand form (Fig. 5-20).

Match Procedures

The procedures used in freestyle sparring in training sessions should be the same as those used in tournament competition. Rules may differ slightly between tournaments but the main points are the same.

1. The sparring area is a twenty-four-foot square.

2. Players face each other in the center of the ring about six feet apart, where they bow first to the referee and then to one another.

3. When the referee says, "Take fighting stance," each player will assume the stance of his or her choice. Then the referee will say, "Begin fighting" (or the Oriental equivalent). Sometimes, instead of giving a verbal command, a referee may elect to merely drop his upraised hand as the starting signal. The players will be told what kind of signal to expect before the match begins.

4. The match will end after three minutes, or when one of the players gains a three point advantage (e.g., 3-0, 4-1, 5-2), whichever comes first. If the score is tied after three minutes, the referee will stop the action just long enough to tell the players they are entering into overtime and a "sudden victory" situation. That is, the first player to score a point wins.

5. A point is scored when a controlled punch, strike, or kick contacts a vital area such as the head, neck, groin, or kidneys. For gymnasium sparring contact must be light. In amateur tournaments the contact will be light-to-medium, with no facial contact below the brown belt level. With beginners no contact of any kind is advised. They should stop their blows about an inch or two from their targets. When the instructor is satisfied with their control they can proceed to light contact. In classroom situations the instructor should vary the rules according to the players' experience.

6. In tournaments, besides the head referee there will be four side judges. Students can be used as side judges in training classes, and at the same time pick up some valuable experience. If any of the officials thinks a point has been scored, he shouts, "Point" and the action stops. A point must be verified by at least three of the five officials.

7. If a player delivers a blow with such force that it results in swelling or bleeding, he or she is disqualified and loses the match. Abusive or unsportsmanlike conduct is also grounds for disqualification.

8. At the end of a match the players again face each other and simultaneously bow. Then after the referee points to the winner, both players bow toward the referee.

Freestyle Principles

For successful freestyle sparring as well as *actual* self-defense fighting, the karateka should keep several principles in mind.

1. *Relax.* Try to remain calm throughout the entire match.

2. *Think* at all times. Use what you have learned. Don't close your eyes and start flailing your arms.

3. Be *confident*. If you do not have a positive attitude in your ability, you have two strikes against you before the match begins.

4. Fight *your* fight. Fight in a style that allows you to utilize your strong points most effectively, and which at the same time minimizes the opponent's strong points.

5. Use a *variety* of techniques so the opponent won't know what to expect. This, of course, implies developing a wide variety of *abilities* that can be used bilaterally. Some top-notch competitors are known to be kicking specialists or punching specialists, however, each is skilled in many aspects of karate; it is just that they tend to rely most heavily on those techniques they personally find most effective.

6. Try not to develop a "set" pattern or rhythm for delivering blows. Your opponent will break the "code" and use it against you. Similarly, do not make unnecessary movements that give an opponent advance knowledge of a blow. A common example of such "telegraphing" occurs when a karateka draws his hand back *before* delivering a punch. The backward motion tips off the opponent and allows him to either block it or beat the karateka to the punch.

7. Do not hesitate to back up. When an opponent pursues or charges you, he usually exposes himself to a counterattack. To be effective though, the retreat must be a controlled tactic.

8. Maintain a high level of physical *fitness*. Merely knowing how to execute karate techniques is useless for self-defense unless you have the strength, flexibility, agility, and endurance to effectively utilize the skills.

9. If an opponent appears to be out of condition, try to tire him out. Keep him moving and never let him rest. Make him continually either defend himself or be aggressive. If he charges, move to the rear or side-step. Keep loose and relaxed, except for occasional flourishes. When your opponent becomes fatigued he will be helpless.

10. In the heat of battle, especially a close contest, you will seldom execute every technique perfectly. However, the more you practice the techniques either individually, in kata movement, or in prearranged sparring, the closer you will come to perfection in freestyle sparring and actual self-defense situations.

11. Be courteous. At all times respect the worth and value of your opponent as a human being. Of course, when someone actually attacks you

with the obvious intent to cause harm, you aren't expected to strike him softly and say, "Excuse me." You should block the attack and with as few punches or kicks as necessary deal with the attacker so that he or she is no longer a threat to you. This may mean knocking your opponent out, or causing such pain that he is completely demoralized.

Courtesy in a true fighting situation means the karateka does not pursue the attack any further than is required. For instance, if the attacker is writhing in pain on the floor as a result of an expertly delivered kick, you wouldn't continue kicking him. Such behavior is unworthy of a self-respecting karateka and puts him or her in the same category as the attacker. Never abuse your karate skill; it is contrary to the spiritualism that is historically inherent in karate.

To assist the karateka in remembering the most important principles for improving his CRAFT the following acronym is provided:

C - confidence
R - relaxation
A - ability
F - fitness
T - think

For organizational purposes the above principles have been discussed separately. All are, however, interrelated. Strength in one leads to strength in the others. Confidence, for example, allows one to relax. When relaxed, one can think more clearly. Also, having developed one's skills and physical fitness to a high degree through dedicated training helps to instill confidence.

Avoiding Attack

One is advised to fight only when absolutely forced to defend himself. The surest preventative measure is to avoid situations where physical assaults are likely to occur, avoiding high risk neighborhoods and people who have proven themselves to be bullies. Always be alert and observant. Pay particular attention to suspicious persons and unusual situations. Try to develop the ability to sense danger, so you can either avoid it or prepare yourself for action if it can't be avoided. Above all, remember it is easy to find trouble if one seeks it or to find peace if one sincerely wishes it.

However, even an individual who tries to avoid violence may be confronted with physical attack. If such a person has supreme confidence in his defensive abilities, he will normally have the social courage to rapidly leave the scene or to try to "talk his way" out of fighting. In other words, a well-trained person feels so secure that proving himself to anyone, including himself, is unnecessary. This attitude is one of the cornerstones of spirituality in karate.

7 THE FIRST KATA

GENERAL INFORMATION

The karate forms (*kata*) are an integral part of karate training. Resembling highly stylized dance routines, kata were originally used primarily to help one develop smooth transitions between individual karate skills. While sparring with imaginary opponents, the practitioner strove to perfect the various stances, blocks, punches, and kicks, and to do so with strength, speed, technical precision, and beauty of motion. Today the training forms have the same objectives. In addition, they are used as part of the requirements one must meet to advance from one degree of proficiency to another, for example, from first-grade brown belt to first-degree black belt.

Presently there are more than fifty kata. Some are included in the training programs of virtually all karate systems while others are unique to a particular school. Generally, each karate style (school) will have about fifteen kata which its karateka are expected to ultimately master. Some of the forms were developed so long ago their origins are obscured in the mists of time. Others have been devised and introduced rather recently. As might be expected, the kata associated with advancement during the initial stages of training are relatively simple. Complexity and difficulty increase as one proceeds up to and through the black belt degrees.

Most kata contain both slow and fast movements. For practice purposes, though, or just for the fun of it, one may execute an entire kata as fast as possible (maintaining, of course, excellent form). On the other hand, one may execute an entire kata form with very slow movements but with great muscular tension (dynamic tension contractions). The latter are especially effective as "body builders."

Although karate by nature is fundamentally a method of self-defense, it is imbued with a spirit of courtesy, humility, and gentleness. Naturally, the execution of kata reflects these spiritualistic qualities. For instance, each kata begins and ends with a standing ceremonial bow as a token of sincerity and respect for fellow participants. Also, the first technique of every karate form is a defensive (blocking) movement.

The ceremonial bow is executed from an attention stance. As one bends forward at the waist, his eyes continue to focus straight ahead, implying that although the karateka will treat an opponent with courtesy he or she is not foolish enough to offer complete trust. After the initial ceremonial bow, the karateka assumes the "ready" stance. (See Position 1, page 129.) It is from this stance that almost every karate form begins. Upon completion of a kata one also assumes the ready stance. A karateka does not relax in the finishing stance since it is the point of preparation for further movement, either another kata or the final ceremonial bow. In other words, the ending of a kata must be as flawlessly executed as the rest of the routine.

PERFORMANCE POINTS

Before even attempting a kata one must, of course, first acquire a fair amount of skill in performing the individual stances and techniques. Once accomplished, the student is prepared to practice them in a karate form. To guide the beginner in evaluating and improving his kata skills, four chief areas of consideration will be discussed.

Footwork

One should strive to finish a kata at the exact point on the performance line from which he or she began. Because the length of one's steps will vary due to individual differences in leg length, it is impossible to state the exact length a step should be. By careful study of the sequence drawings in this chapter, one can determine the appropriate size step for his size. Angles regarding directions of the steps, however, do not vary. These angles will be stated precisely in the written descriptions.

Stances and Techniques

Every kata consists of a number of stances and techniques, each of which serves a particular function. The karateka must keep in mind that he is fighting an imaginary opponent or opponents and should therefore always be envisioning a target, with each movement having either a defensive or offensive purpose. In the written descriptions that accompany the sequence drawings of the kata presented in this chapter, the meaning or reason for each movement will be explained.

Again, let it be stressed that one must always strive for perfection when performing a kata. This means close attention must be paid to even the smallest details.

Timing

In performing a kata, there must be a pause at each stance. It will be just long enough to permit the accompanying technique to be executed. The karateka will then move to the next stance. Occurring throughout the kate, though, are major pauses of about one second in duration. As one performs the kata, keeping in mind the major pauses, an instructor or the trainee himself will count off the stances (1, 2, 3, 4, etc.).

To simplify the learning process, the beginner is encouraged to *first* step into a stance and *then* execute the technique. Each movement should be distinct and separate. An example may be seen in positions 139 through 144. After the kata movements are learned, the separation in movement between a stance and technique becomes more subtle. An example of this is shown rather well in positions 6 through 12. At this point, precise timing (rhythm) is required to obtain maximal results from the techniques. Timing is chiefly related to the proper summation of forces (page 49).

Breathing

Properly controlled breathing helps a karateka to maintain an attitude or calmness during a kata and to execute techniques more powerfully. Usually the most effective breathing pattern is achieved when one concentrates on exhaling during the delivery of a technique (block or blow). Forceful exhalations are produced by powerful contractions of the expiratory muscles, chiefly the diaphragm, and the muscles of the abdomen and thorax (rib cage). As a result of the contractions, a more powerful blow can be delivered because the thorax, to which the chest and arm muscles attach, is made more stable. Besides, strongly contracted abdominal muscles keep the karateka's upper body from being pushed rearward at the moment of contact (see action-reaction, page 53). Again, the result is a more powerful blow.

At a precisely scheduled time near the mid-point of many kata, a loud yell is emitted by the karateka (see position 63 in the sequence drawings). bin more complex kata such a shout, called "kiai" (pronounced "kee-eye"), may be released at more than one point. Always, though, it is issued at the precise moment of imaginary contact.

The actual sound of the kiai yell varies according to individual preferences. "ki" is common, along with such noises as "zut," "who," "chew," "yo," and "hi." Often, the sounds have a hissing quality since the air is being forced out from the lungs very rapidly.

The values of kiai are related to the forceful expulsion of air, which was discussed previously. In addition to the physical and mechanical aspects, however, the scream gives the karateka a psychological advantage since it is quite unnerving to an opponent who is not familiar with it. Kiai also helps the karateka to focus his or her energies, both physical and mental, into a concentrated effort at the moment of contact. In a kata this may not seem significant until one remembers that one of the purposes of kata training is preparation for combat.

GUIDE TO USING THE SEQUENCE DRAWINGS

This section has been included to help the learner use the sequence drawings in this chapter effectively. The drawings were made directly from selected frames taken from movies of karate champion Bill Wallace as he performed the first karate form (pinan-chodan, Korean style). In most other karate styles the first form differs only slightly.

A large number of positions, 150 in all, were chosen to provide complete clarity of movement thus eliminating much of the confusion that is generally experienced by beginners. For each position both a front and back view are shown, with the back views located directly beneath the corresponding front views. Camera locations for taking the front and back view movies are indicated in Fig. 7-1.

Figure 7-1 also contains a diagram that may help the beginning karateka to understand the proper direction of movement during the first form. Facing the front view camera, the model begins at position 1, and then moves to position 17. He then proceeds back to the starting point, which is also number 34. Next, he takes four steps directly toward the front view camera to position 63. After pivoting 270° counter-clockwise, he goes to position 79. From this point he returns to position 99. The karateka then takes four steps directly toward the back view camera which places him again at the starting spot (120). Upon turning 270° counter-clockwise, he steps forward at a 45 degree angle to position 132. Pivoting 135 degrees to position 138, he steps at a 45-degree angle to position 144. Finally, he finishes the movement by stepping back to position 150. At this terminating point the karateka should be on the exact spot and in the identical stance as in position 1.

The pinan chodan kata provides an opportunity for the student to practice the ready, forward, and back stances, as well as several stance changes. He also practices, with both hands, the four basic blocks (low, middle, high, and knife-hand) and the lunge punch.

In the initial stages of learning, the kata should be divided into several parts. The exact number depends upon an individual's learning capacity. After the first part is learned, the second is added, then the third and so on. With each new addition one should start at the beginning of the kata and incorporate the new part. To assist the karateka in determining the proper pace for the kata, each new stance is indicated by a circle number above the appropriate figure. A number encircled twice indicates major (one second) pauses.

Descriptions of Sequence Drawings

Written descriptions accompany the sequence drawings of the kata. They are necessary to point out factors that are difficult or impossible to show in the drawings. For instance, times for inhaling and exhaling are noted, and body weight distribution is discussed when deemed necessary. The name of each stance and technique is also stated, and hand forms and movements are further clarified. When the sequence drawings are referred to in the written descriptions, the *number* of the shecific position will be used.

For the sake of brevity, not every relevant aspect of each movement (e.g., 29-34) is discussed. Since many of the movements in the kata are repetitive, different points are discussed with each repetition. Therefore, by studying the entire kata one can acquire a complete picture. For additional clarification, one can refer to the presentation of individual stances and techniques in Chapter five.

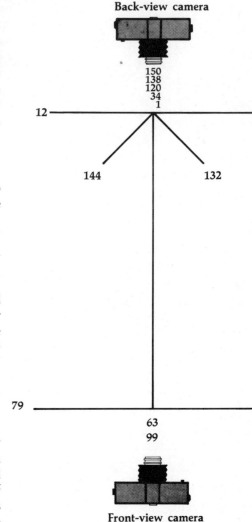

Fig. 7-1.
Directional floor plan for the first (also called pinan chodan or Heian shodan) kata. Numbers on the diagram refer to position numbers in the sequence drawings. Also shown are front and back view camera locations, from which the footage was taken for the sequence drawings.

F

B

(1)   (2)   (3)   (4)   (5)   (6)

From the *ready stance* (1), the karateka pivots counterclockwise on the balls of his right foot. Then he shifts his weight to the rear (3)–(4) and brings his left foot back to his right to assume the *ready stance* (5). He inhales during the entire movement (1)–(5). Most of his weight is on the balls of the feet in (5).

F

(7)   (8)   (9)   (10)   (11)   (12)

B

This allows the karateka to easily step forward into a left *forward stance* (10) and to execute a left *low block* (12). Preceding every blocking movement, his hands should pass through the *knife-hand* phase; note positions (7)–(10). Exhalation occurs throughout the entire movement (7)–(12).

F

(13)   (14)   (15)   (16)   (17)

B

The karateka inhales as he steps from (12) to a right *forward stance* (17). During the step, his right knee points outward and his right heel passes close to his left heel. The movement is seen from a clearer perspective in (53). He inhales during (13)–(15) and exhales during (16)–(17).

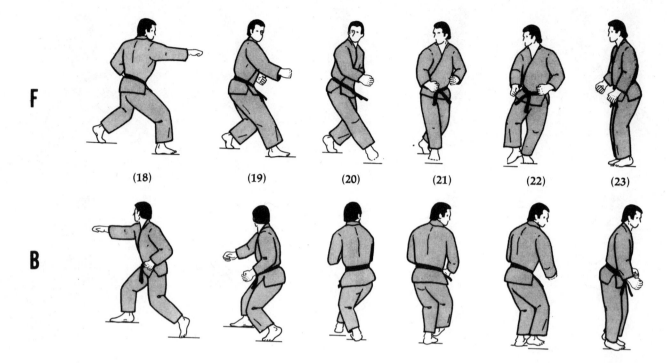

F

B

(18) (19) (20) (21) (22) (23)

From (17) the karateka shifts his weight
rearward (18) and, after first looking
over his right shoulder, begins a 180°
pivot on his left foot. Once lifted (20),
his right foot does not touch the floor
until he places it next to his left in the
ready stance (23). Inhalation occurs
throughout the entire movement.

F

(24)   (25)   (26)   (27)   (28)   (29)

B

One steps from position (23) to a right *forward stance* and executes a right *low block* (29). Again, note that his hands pass through a *knife-hand* phase (26)–(27). Exhalation takes places throughout the entire movement (24)–(29).

F

(30) (31) (32) (33) (34)

B

From (29), the karateka shifts his weight forward (30) and steps to a left *forward stance* to deliver a *lunge punch* (34). The step, followed by a forward rotation of the left hip and shoulder (33) and the extension of the left arm and wrist rotation, results in considerable force being developed. He inhales during (30)–(32), and exhales from (33) to (34).

F   (35)   (36)   (37)   (38)   (39)

B

Pivoting on the ball of his right foot, the karateka turns 90° to his left to assume a *ready stance* (39). As with every turn, he looks in the appropriate direction before turning his body. He inhales during (35)–(39).

F

(40)   (41)   (42)   (43)   (44)   (45)

B

The karateka's weight is on the balls of his feet in (39) so he can step forward smoothly to a left *forward stance* and execute a left *low block* (45). The palm of the *knife-hand* position in (41)–(43) is facing downward. In the *forward stance* position, his rear leg is fully extended. He exhales during the entire movement (40)–(45).

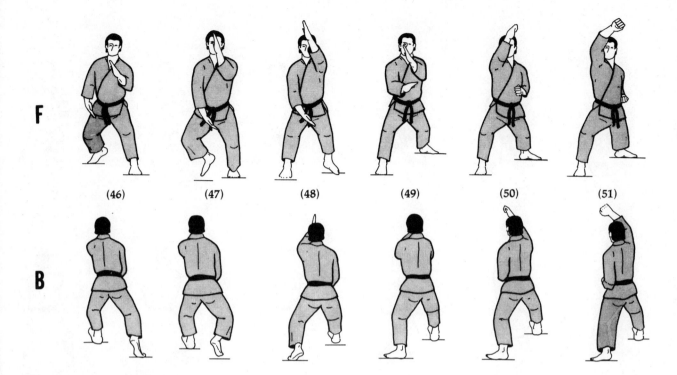

F

(46)   (47)   (48)   (49)   (50)   (51)

B

From (45), the karateka steps forward into a right *forward stance* (49) and executes a right *high block* (51). Both palms face inward (46)–(49) and immediately after (49) his hands form fists. Also, see positions (56) and (62). He inhales from (46)–(48) and exhales from (49)–(51).

F

B

(52) (53) (54) (55) (56) (57)

Shifting his weight forward (52), the karateka steps into a left *forward stance* (55) and performs a left *high block* with his left arm (57). By pointing his left knee and toe outward and bringing his left heel close to the other (53), he is able to step forward more rapidly than normal (see page 47). He inhales during (52)–(54) and exhales during (55)–(57).

F

(58)   (59)   (60)   (61)   (62)   (63)

B

This step to a right *forward stance* and *high block* is almost identical to that shown in (46)–(51). In both cases, the karateka brings his elbows very close together as they pass between (61)–(62). The right arm is forcefully raised to (63) in a blocking movement. The karateka inhales from (58)–(61) and exhales from (62)–(63). KIAI at (63).

F

(64) (65) (66) (67) (68) (69)

B

Shifting his weight to the right foot, the karateka pivots 270° to the left to a *back stance* (69). Once lifted, the left foot does not touch the floor until its final placement (68). Again, notice that the karateka's head turns before his body makes its move (65). Inhalation occurs between (64) and (69).

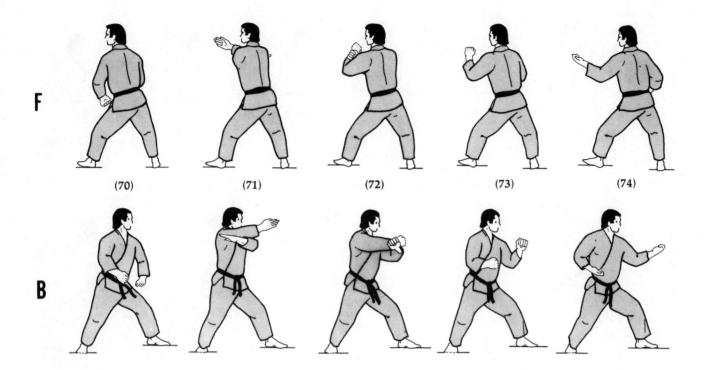

F

(70) (71) (72) (73) (74)

B

Remaining in the *back stance* (70), the karateka executes a left *middle inside block* (74). As always, before the block, the hands pass through the *knife-hand* phase (71). In the *back stance* about 70% of his weight is on the rear foot. Exhalation takes place throughout the entire movement (70)–(74).

(75)   (76)   (77)   (78)   (79)

F

B

From (74) the karateka shifts his weight to the left foot so he can more easily step into a right *forward stance* (78) and deliver a *lunge punch* (79). Bringing his left arm forcefully to the rear (77)–(79) helps him to drive his right arm forward with greater force. He inhales during (75)–(77) and exhales during (78)–(79).

| (80) | (81) | (82) | (83) | (84) | (85) |

The karateka shifts his weight back to the ball of his left foot (80)–(81) and pivots $180°$ to a *back stance* (85). His right foot moves from (81) to (85) in one movement, without touching the floor. Again, in a *back stance*, 70% of his weight is on the rear foot. He inhales during (80)–(85).

| F | (86) | (87) | (88) | (89) | (90) | (91) |

| B |

Remaining in the *back stance* (86), the karateka executes a right *middle inside block* (91). The movement is the same as that shown in (70)–(74) except one is a left-hand block (74) and the other is a right-hand block (91). Note the *knife-hand* phase (87)–(88). Exhalation occurs throughout the entire movement (86)–(91).

F

(92)   (93)   (94)   (95)   (96)

B

Stepping to a *forward stance* (95), the karateka delivers a left *lunge punch* (96). Again the summation of forces (discussed with drawings (30)–(34)) and the forceful bringing back of the opposing arm (94)–(96) (as in drawings (75)–(79)) produce a powerful punch. The karateka inhales from (92)–(94) and exhales from (95)–(96).

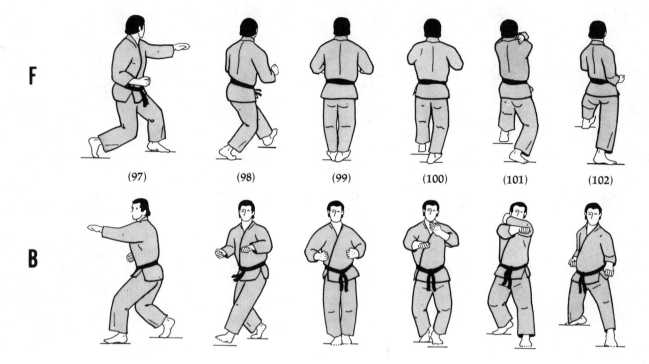

F

(97)   (98)   (99)   (100)   (101)   (102)

B

First pivoting 90° to assume a *ready stance* (99), the karateka then steps to a *forward stance* and performs a left *low block* (102). As his hands pass through the *knife-hand* phase, notice how the right side of his neck is protected (101). He inhales during (97)–(99) and exhales during (100)–(102).

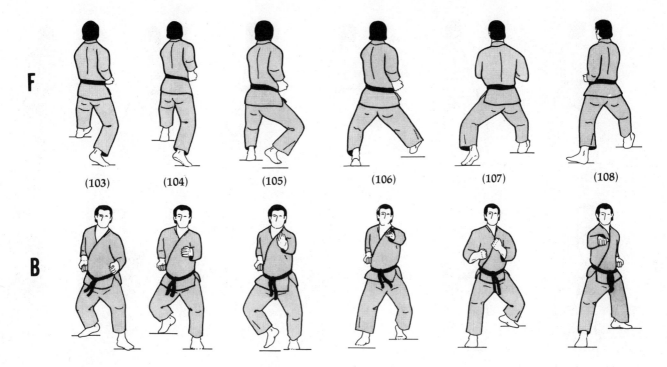

F

(103)　　(104)　　(105)　　(106)　　(107)　　(108)

B

From (102), the karateka steps to a right *forward stance* and delivers a *lunge punch* (108). As with all such punches, the rear leg is forcefully extended in accordance with the physical principle concerning action-reaction (see page 53). He inhales during (103)–(106) and exhales during (107)–(108).

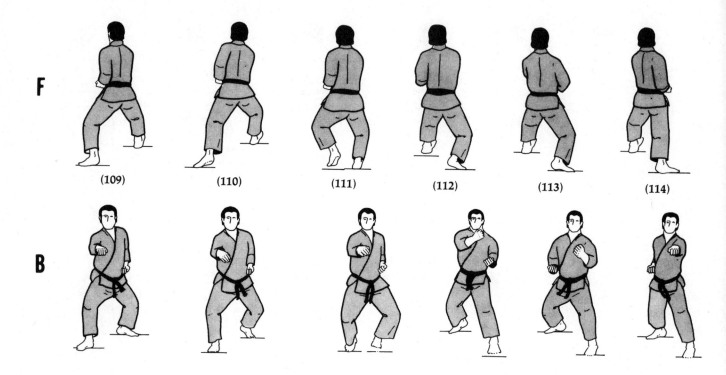

F (109)   (110)   (111)   (112)   (113)   (114)

B

Shifting his weight forward onto his right foot (110), the karateka steps to a left *forward stance* and delivers a left *lunge punch* (114). Again, observe the way the left foot is brought forward (110)–(112). Note the *knife-hand* position in (110)–(111). He inhales during (109)–(112) and exhales during (113)–(114).

F (115) (116) (117) (118) (119) (120)

B

The karateka shifts his weight onto his left foot, steps to a right *forward stance*, and delivers a right *lunge punch* (120). Note that he is looking directly at his imaginary target. This is important for all blows. He inhales during (115)–(118) and exhales during (119)–(120).

F (121) (122) (123) (124) (125) (126)

B

The karateka pivots 270° to his left on the ball of his right foot to a *back stance* (125) and executes a *knife-hand block* (126). His left wrist rotates from a palm-up to a palm-down position from (125)–(126). The left elbow is bent a bit at (126). He inhales during (121)–(124) and exhales during (125)–(126).

F

(127) (128) (129) (130) (131) (132)

B

From (126), the karateka steps 45° to his right to a *back stance* (130) and executes a right *knife-hand block* (132). Both hands remain in the *knife-hand* form from (126)–(132). Note that he looks to his right (128) before his body moves in that direction. He inhales during (127)–(130) and exhales during (131)–(132).

F

(133)   (134)   (135)   (136)   (137)   (138)

B

Shifting his weight rearward (133), the karateka pivots 135° on the ball of his right foot and assumes a *back stance* (136). From this stance, he performs a right *knife-hand* block (138). As usual, he looks before turning his body. He inhales during (133)–(136) and exhales during (137)–(138).

F

(139) (140) (141) (142) (143) (144)

B

From (138), the karateka steps 45° to the left to a *back stance* (141) and executes a *knife-hand* block with his left hand (144). Both feet remain *flat* on the floor from (141) through (144). Inhalation occurs during (139)–(142); exhalation occurs from (143)–(144).

(145) (146) (147) (148) (149) (150)

Merely performing a kata with mechanical accuracy is not enough. It must be mastered to the extent that the karateka can perform it with "feeling." That is, he should concentrate on visualizing imaginary opponents so when he executes a block it is as if he is actually blocking a blow, and when he delivers a blow it is as if he is actually striking an opponent. *Total* concentration is required. In addition, one should strive to ultimately reach the point where he experiences a beautiful kinesthetic feeling as he moves powerfully and gracefully through the entire kata. Much practice and attention to detail is required in mastering a kata; however, the rewards are well worth the effort.

For the final movement of the kata, the karateka pivots 45° to the left on the ball of his right foot to a *ready stance* (150). His left foot moves from (145) to (149) in one smooth motion. If, during the entire kata, the karateka has taken steps of precise lengths and directions, at position (150) he should be in exactly the same spot where he began the kata in position (1). He inhales during (145)–(148) and exhales during (149)–(150).

GLOSSARY

Throughout this book the Anglicized versions of the karate terms have been used. However, many schools prefer to use the traditional Oriental terminology. In this glossary the English words are listed first, followed by their Japanese and Korean equivalents. The Oriental words are spelled with the Roman alphabet according to the way they sound. Translations, therefore, do differ, especially since some of the sounds have no precise English equivalents.

English	Japanese	Korean
Attention	Kio tsuke	Cha-ryut
Begin	Ha jime	Si-jak
Black belter	Yu-dan-sha	Yoo-dan-ja
Block (ing)	Uke	Makki (Bahng ha)
Blocks, types of		
high block	jodan uke	sang-dan makki
knife-hand block	chudan-shuto uke	soo-do makki
low block	gedan-barai uke	ha-dan (naeryo) makki
middle block	chudan uke	chung-dan makki
X-block	juji uke	gah-ro makki
Body, parts of		
arm	wan	pal
ball of foot	chusoku	ap-bal-cumchi
elbow	hiji	pal-koop
face	kao	ol-gul
forearm	ude	pal-mok
head	atama	mur-ree
heel	kakato	twit-bal-cumchi
instep	haisoku	bal-tung
knee	hiza	moo-roop
wrist	koken	pal-mok
Bow	Rei	In-sa
Buddhistic meditation	Zen	Sun
Contest	Shiai	Si-hap
Examination	Shinsa	Simsa
Fighting (empty hand)	Karate	Tae-kwon-do
First form	Heian shodan	Pinan-chodan

Form	Kata	Hyong
Front	Mae	Ap
Kick (ing)	Kere	chagee
Kicks, types of		
back kick	ushiro geri	twi chagee
front kick	mae geri	ap chagee
hook kick	kake geri	yang-chok (foo-rio) chagee
roundhouse kick	mawashi geri	dol-rio chagee
side kick	yoko geri	yop chagee
stamping kick	ushiro fumikomi	pal-twi-chok chagee
Knife-hand	Shuto	Soo-do (sudo)
Left	Hidari	Wen-chok
Master instructor	Shidan	Sa-bum-nim
Meditation	Mokuso	Mook-yom
Non-black belter	Mu-dan-sha	Moo-dan-ja
Numbers		
one	ichi	il
two	ni	ee
three	san	sam
four	shi	sah
five	go	o
six	roku	yook
seven	shichi	chil
eight	hachi	pal
nine	ku	koo
ten	ju	ship
eleven	ju-ichi	ship-il
twenty	ni-ju	ee-ship
twenty-one	ni-ju-ichi	ee-ship-il
thirty	san-ju	sam-ship
Opponent	Aite	Sang-dae-bang
Performance line	Embusan	Chun-bee-sun
Player	Shen-shu	Sun-soo
Practice hall	Dojo	Dojang
Punch	Tsuki	Chigee
Ready	Junbi	Chun-bee
Rear	Ushiro	Twi
Right	Migi	Ba-run-jok
Side	Yoko	Yup
Sparring	Kumite	Tae-ryon
Stance	Dachi	sugi
Stances, types of		
attention stance	heisoku dachi	moa sugi
back stance	kokutsu dachi	hugul (foo-ku) sugi
cat stance	neko-ashi dachi	twi-pal sugi
forward stance	zenkutsu dachi	chon-gul sugi
horse stance	kiba dachi	kima sugi
hour-glass stance	sanchin dachi	ol-gul-yo sugi
pigeon-toe stance	uchi-hachiji dachi	ko-chung sugi
ready stance	hachiji dachi	chun-bee sugi
Strike	Uchi	Tae-rigee

Strikes and punches,
    types of
    back fist strike   ubaken uchi   yop-tae-rigee
    forefist punch   chudan-choku zuki   chung-dan-chigee
    inverted fist strike   sayu uchi   naeryo-tae-rigee
    knife-hand strike   shuto uchi   sudo-tae-rigee
    lunge punch   oi zuki   paro-chigee
    reverse punch   gyaki zuki   pan-dae-chigee
Striking board   Makiwara   Tal-yon-chu
Striking surfaces,
    hands
    back fist   uraken   ree-kwon
    fore fist   seiken   chon-kwon
    hammer fist   kentsui   yug-kwon
    knife-hand   shuto   soo-do (sudo)
    palm heel   teisho   chang-kwon
    ridge-hand   haito   yok-sudo
    spear finger   nukite   kwon-soo
Striking surfaces,
    legs and feet
    ball of foot   chusoku   ap-bal-cumchi
    foot edge   sokuto   chok-do
    heel   kakato   twi-pal-cumchi
    instep   haisoku   bal-tung
    knee   hiza   moo-roop
Teacher   Sensei   Sa-bum
Technique   Waza   Ki-sul
Time   Jikan   Si-ban
Uniform, karate   Karate gi   Dobok
Vital point   Kyu-sho   Yup-soo
Yell   Kiai   Ki-hap

INDEX